From One Light, Many Colors

Understanding God's Design
for Racial Unity

by
Silas Johnson

HARRISON HOUSE
Tulsa, Oklahoma

From One Light, Many Colors:
Understanding God's Design for Racial Unity
ISBN 0-89274-987-3
Copyright © 1996 by Silas Johnson
Full Counsel Ministries
P. O. Box 2160
North Little Rock, Arkansas 72115

Published by Harrison House, Inc.
P. O. Box 35035
Tulsa, Oklahoma 74153

Dedication

I want to dedicate this book to the *apple of my eye*, my help meet and companion of twenty-two years, Jennifer, without whose encouragement this book would not have been possible.

Contents

Introduction

1   Nation Against Nation   11

2   The Danger of Overemphasizing Racial Differences 21

3   Sound Doctrine vs. Genealogies   29

4   Lawful Use of the Law   47

5   Reconciliation — The Great Truth   59

6   The Restitution of All Things   75

7   Hypocrisy — Seed of Racism   91

8   Heirs Together of God's Grace   113

9   Where to From Here?   127

Introduction

As we head into the twenty-first century, we are faced with many challenging, complex and sensitive issues. Of these issues, none is more urgent to the Church and to the world at large than that of ethnic strife and division.

People have groped and wrestled with this problem for years. With countless hours and dollars and even lives being spent toward resolving it, the results have been, at best, superficial or tokenistic in nature.

As we near the end of this age, most political officials agree that we are sitting on a powder keg with a lit fuse. It's like being in the midst of an earthquake with increasingly fractured fault lines. The pressure cooker has passed the boiling point, and it's sending off an ominous steam of churning unrest and turmoil.

Unfortunately, in the Church, as in society as a whole, the issue of race has been labeled by some as "too hot to handle." It has been relegated to the "back burner" by others and is stirred only occasionally. Still others have covered it with a heavy lid and left it to simmer.

From South Central Los Angeles to Bosnia, from Palestine to Northern Ireland, there has been a churning of ethnic, cultural and religious strife, hatred and bigotry. Having been harbored for years, ethnic strife is again active and ready to erupt in volcanic proportions.

In America, we have "progressed" from Martin Luther King, Jr. to Rodney King, with all civil, social, political and even religious efforts falling short of solving this problem, a problem which has existed since the Tower of Babel.

Indeed, in spite of man's best and most noble efforts, we find ourselves back at "square one" with the same old rhetoric — the same fears, the same accusations and, naturally, the same futile results that we have gotten for years.

We must defuse this powder keg.

We must close the fault lines of this devastating earthquake.

We must relieve the tensions of this seething pressure cooker which threatens us with violence and upheaval not known since the beginning of time.

To do this, we must put forth some real answers, and we must do it now.

The only answer to this crisis is truth. The only real truth is found in the Book of Truth — the Bible. The great truth of the Bible is Jesus, the Christ.

For too long we, even in the Church, have trivialized and sloganized the all-important and universal truth that Jesus was anointed of God to be the Answer to *every* problem that confronts mankind. Religion has veiled and isolated Christ in such a way that Christianity has become a "religious faith" instead of a practical way of living and handling every aspect of life.

In this book it will be irrefutably demonstrated that Christ Jesus is anointed of God to be the Answer to all racial and ethnic differences among men. He indeed is **the way, the truth, and the life** (John 14:6).

Because truth is confronting, it will be controversial to those who are contrary. But to those who are contrite, this book will serve as a treatise to bring forth the humbling but sobering truth that Christ Jesus is the only Common Denominator for solving all the equations of life. He is the only Common Thread in the tapestry of racial diversity. He is the only Mediator Who has the right and ability to represent all people before God and then to reconcile all people to each other.

If the Church will receive this revelation and preach it to all nations as a witness, people of all races will truly know the blessedness of dwelling together in unity.

Some would say that difficult, complex problems demand difficult, complex answers. This is not true.

We are warned by the apostle Paul in Second Corinthians 11:3 not to be beguiled from the simplicity which is in the anointed Jesus. The word *simplicity* means "singleness," "sincerity."[1] It means purity or that from which all else is drawn, fit together, joined or hinged upon.

Christ Jesus must remain our focus. All else then becomes subject, secondary and subordinate to Him.

A problem or issue is merely something that is attempting to exalt itself above the knowledge of Christ (God) (2 Corinthians 10:5). Every problem is a result of carnal, fleshly thinking or indulgence by which people have been beguiled or corrupted from the simplicity (singleness, sincerity, purity and preeminence) of Christ.

If one is to understand and ultimately embrace this writer's approach in dealing with the issues discussed in this book, a revelation of the simplicity of Christ is essential. No matter how vast, diverse and divergent God's creation and creatures may be, as stated before, Christ Jesus is the only Common Thread of it all. He must, of necessity and right, receive all the glory. This cannot be compromised.

Such exaltation of Christ as the Answer has always been controversial and will be no less controversial in this book.

---

[1]James H. Strong, "Greek Dictionary of the New Testament, "*Strong's Exhaustive Concordance of the Bible* (Nashville: Abingdon 1890), p. 14, #572.

The preaching of Christ means that no flesh is able to glory or boast. This humbling but sobering truth is the common denominator for solving all the equations of life.

This great truth will be found unacceptable by some; however, it will certainly be found indisputable by all.

1

Nation Against Nation

And as he sat upon the mount of Olives, the
disciples came unto him privately, saying, Tell us,
when shall these things be? and what shall be the sign
of thy coming, and of the end of the world?

And Jesus answered and said unto them, Take heed
that no man deceive you.

For many shall come in my name, saying, I am
Christ; and shall deceive many.

And ye shall hear of wars and rumours of wars: see
that ye be not troubled: for all these things must come
to pass, but the end is not yet.

For nation shall rise against nation, and kingdom
against kingdom: and there shall be famines, and
pestilences, and earthquakes, in divers places.

All these are the beginning of sorrows.

Matthew 24:3-8

When asked by His disciples concerning signs that
would indicate the end times, Jesus spoke forth this
prophetic discourse from Matthew, chapter 24.

Notice He said one of the primary signs of the end of
this age would be an increase in wars and strife between
nations.

The word *nation* in verse 7 is the Greek word,
pronounced *eth'-nos,* which means "race, tribe or people."[1]
It is the word from which we derive the term *ethnic,*[2] and

---

[1]James H. Strong. *Strong's Exhaustive Concordance,* Compact Ed. (Grand Rapids: Baker, 1992), "Greek Dictionary of the New Testament," p. 25, #1484.

[2]*Webster's New World College Dictionary,* 3d ed., s.v. "ethnic."

thus ethnic group. So this end-time strife should not be construed as wars between countries only, but also wars between ethnic groups, races, tribes and peoples.

We need only to take a brief look around the globe to see the fulfillment of this prophecy. Rwanda, Bosnia, Northern Ireland and, of course, the Middle East are just a few examples of this violent and dramatic struggle between different ethnic groups.

Here in America, in spite of all the laws to end segregation and discrimination, there is a renewed tension brewing. The diverse ethnic groups are groping over their piece of the "American Dream" pie, which is rapidly running out of slices.

Nations as a whole are making shifts in their economy, government and military to deal with an evolving international community. Yet at the same time, the ethnic communities within these nations are polarizing more and more.

Unfortunately, this diversion and polarization of ethnic groups is also affecting the Church. As more people are searching for identity, purpose and historical heritage in all races, there has been an increased tendency toward focusing on differences in ethnicity and a resistance to homogenizing the culture. Driven by pride, fear, ignorance and even hatred, the races are pulling apart.

Caught in the midst of this windstorm, the Church must decide whether to follow the flow of society or set the standard for society to follow. If we are to be obedient to our Lord, we must choose the latter. As Jesus said in Matthew's gospel:

> **Ye are the salt of the earth: but if the salt have lost his savour, wherewith shall it be salted? it is thenceforth good for nothing, but to be cast out, and to be trodden under foot of men.**

Ye are the light of the world. A city that is set on an
hill cannot be hid.

Neither do men light a candle, and put it under a
bushel, but on a candlestick; and it giveth light unto all
that are in the house.

Let your light so shine before men, that they may
see your good works, and glorify your Father which is
in heaven.

Matthew 5:13-16

As we approach the twenty-first century, many groups,
philosophers and idealogists are jockeying for positions of
leadership in our world. Jesus warned us that if we lose our
salt, then we lose our distinction as the moral and spiritual
leaders of the world. If we no longer provide moral and
spiritual leadership, then we are good for nothing and will
be trodden underfoot by a stampeding herd. As the saying
goes, "Lead — get out of the way — or get run over."

There will be many groups and individuals arguing for
leadership in solving the problem of ethnic strife. But their
carnal, fleshly methods cannot provide any lasting solution.

The Church has the anointing to provide the leadership
in this area. But if we continue to follow the pattern of the
world and flow with winds of popular culture, as we have
in the past, we will abdicate our leadership to the false
christs of our world.

To understand this age-old problem, we must first take
a panoramic view of our world, then focus in on our nation
and on the Church. Let's take a look at where we are now
and why past methods have failed.

The Decline of the Superpowers

For almost fifty years, until the fall of the Iron Curtain,
the attention of the whole world was upon the ideological
battle between the two great superpowers, the U.S.A. and

the Soviet Union; as well as their ideologies, capitalism and communism, respectively. It was indeed a long, expensive Cold War that caused most of the nations of the world to become aligned in one camp or the other.

These two superpowers were so dominant that all other ethnic and cultural battles, with the possible exception of the Middle East, seemed insignificant. The threat of a common foe and the need to propagate these major ideologies consumed the limelight, suppressing racial and ethnic differences.

But many failed to realize that the political expedience, financial advantage and military coalitions were only as lasting as the crisis was which brought about their necessity. When that crisis was over, so were the relationships.

With the light no longer shining on those two world superpowers, the difference and diversity of nations is beginning to resurface.

Almost immediately with the breakup of the Soviet Union, the ethnic and religious hatred, which had been simmering like a pressure cooker for years, exploded into the face of the world.

The former Yugoslavia has been torn apart by the war between the Bosnians and Serbs. Differences that had been suppressed but never resolved spilled over into violence.

America, no longer unified by the common foe of communism, is now having the seams of its multicultural tapestry tested by the upheaval of "special-interest groups" of all kinds. Nations which strained themselves financially to promote their ideals abroad are being bankrupted through their efforts to promote multifaceted ideals at home.

A Search for Identity

No longer motivated by a common cause, people of the '90s — both sexes, all races and various socioeconomic groups — are searching for an identity. Because of their innate demand for acceptance, respect and recognition, their search for identity portends an earthquake of strife and division. This upheaval will test to the very core the phrase of our pledge of allegiance: "...one nation, under God, indivisible, with liberty and justice for all."

As we shall discuss later, the Church has not been exempted from this identity search; and our theme of **one Lord, one faith, one baptism** (Ephesians 4:5) is likewise being tested.

The lesson we must learn here is that, when there is no cause or when the cause is no longer deemed worthy, people will turn and search for identity. The extreme of this occurs when finding that identity *becomes* the cause. This is the fiber from which strife is born and wars are made. Extreme ethnicity, racism and bigotry are always the results of such pursuits.

When people divide along racial or ethnic lines, the next step is to establish a leader or leadership structure. Leaders by nature are protective of their domains, so they set up what amounts to kingdoms. Hence, we see the progression of which Jesus spoke in this Scripture verse from Matthew, chapter 24:

> **For nation shall rise against nation, and kingdom against kingdom: and there shall be famines, and pestilences, and earthquakes, in divers places.**
> **Matthew 24:7**

Ethnic group against ethnic group escalates into kingdom against kingdom. Thus we see the cycle of man:

a. Man searches for identity.

b. Man is united by a cause.

c. Every cause has a leader, its "christ."

d. Every leader builds a kingdom.

This cycle is not inherently bad. It is God Who makes man after this fashion. God wants man to discover his identity, submit to something bigger than himself, become subject to leadership and then do his or her part in building *the* kingdom.

The problem is, this principle can be used for evil as well as for good. The wrong leader with wrong motives can lead people in the wrong direction, and even the *right* leader with wrong motives can be disastrous. As Jesus said:

> **Take heed that no man deceive you.**
>
> **For many shall come in my name, saying, I am Christ** (the Anointed One[3])**; and shall deceive many.**
> **Matthew 24:4,5**

These are antichrists or false christs. They say they are sent. They say they have the answers. But they are only out to build their own kingdoms.

Look at the false christs of our day: the political, social and religious ideologies which promise much but deliver little. They promise peace and safety, but it does not occur.

The United Nations claims to be anointed to bring unity, but they want to do it by taking away identity. In contrast, Adolph Hitler rallied people around the cause of a superior race. Communism promised equality to everyone. Even democracy, with its high ideals of freedom for all, cannot satisfactorily fulfill its claims in the absence of personal responsibility.

It was God, Who created and gave purpose to all the diverse and divergent cultures and groups on the earth. Only He and His Christ, the Lord Jesus, together with the Church, can provide the answer to this complex problem. It is only in Christ Jesus that mankind can find identity, cause,

---

[3]Some comments within the text and insertions within Scripture are based on Kenneth Copeland's teaching of the anointing.

king and kingdom. Jesus is the One anointed of God to provide this for the whole world.

We can understand how the world does not have this revelation. But the sad thing is that the Church does not have it either.

A Problem of Division

This brings us to one of the main concerns of this book. I am greatly troubled that many brethren in the Black community are looking in the wrong place for their identity. Even worse, some have made the search for identity a cause. This cause has necessitated leaders, and these leaders have started to build kingdoms.

Right in the middle of the greatest move of God's Spirit that mankind has ever seen, Satan is doing his best to divide the Church and thus to hinder the anointing of God. As we shall discuss later, this is a clever diversion to hinder us from focusing on *the cause* — the Gospel of Christ.

The world will not believe we are sent if we are not as one. Perhaps the whole world would have accepted Christ Jesus years ago if all of Israel had accepted Him as the Messiah or the Anointed One. But some did not believe and even fought against Him. The Roman rulers of that day were confused, and it hindered their faith, because God's people were divided and even fighting each other.

Not only will people not believe, but this lack of unity will hinder the anointing to receive healing, deliverance and supply. We must let the world know that there is a common identity, a common cause, a common leader and a common kingdom of which we can all be a part, regardless of our diverse backgrounds. Notice this Scripture says:

> **There is one body, and one Spirit, even as ye are called in one hope of your calling;**
>
> **One Lord, one faith, one baptism,**

One God and Father of all, who is above all, and through all, and in you all.

Ephesians 4:4-6

This revelation literally causes Satan to tremble, because it strips him of his greatest tools of control, deception and manipulation. But if we keep walking in carnality and after the flesh, we will remain divided and powerless. This attitude is anti-anointing or anti-Christ. No spirit that causes Christians to divide is of God. **Is Christ divided?** (1 Corinthians 1:13a). No! God forbid.

Carnal Methods of Control

For too long in the Church we have attempted to use carnal methods to deal with racial diversity. In the world, three primary methods have been employed to manage the races:

•**Oppression**   •**Suppression**   •**Concession**

Let's consider each of these methods.

• Oppression

Oppression is the principle of racial supremacy. One race presumes to be dominant over all others and develops the doctrine, justification and support systems necessary to propagate its tenants. Fear and deception are the main forces behind this method.

Oftentimes, the proponents of oppressive racial tactics believe they are honoring God by enforcing this system of separation and preserving the "purity" of the races. Therefore, the end justifies the means.

History as well as God's Word lets us know that oppression is demonic and will ultimately be overthrown. Hitler's Nazi Party is an example of this.

• Suppression

Suppression is the attempt to minimize differences in ethnic groups through the force of law, government or social engineering. This artificial method is quickly exposed as soon as the restraints are removed.

As we previously stated, as soon as communism fell, the ethnic strife in Yugoslavia came to the surface.

Quota systems, tokenism and other methods simply placate the race problem; they do not resolve it.

• Concession

Then there is concession. We see this largely in America. Pressure had been brought about due to guilt associated with past injustices, and ongoing accusations. In order to keep peace, and diffuse hostility, concessions are made. This is a system of politics, expedience and correctness rather than true reconciliation.

Concession is the result of overcharged democracy, with liberty being pushed to the extreme. As deep as the pockets of democratic liberality may be, it can be bankrupted by too many special-interest groups. Everyone cannot have their own little kingdom. We cannot re-invent the wheel for everyone's wagon.

As America continues to make concessions to every special group, it drifts further into division and strife. Will we go to a Black History Month, an Indian History Month, an Hispanic History Month and a month for any other racial group to the degree that we no longer have time for American history? The extreme pursuit of personal liberty is the greatest threat to the ideal of national freedom.

A Challenge to the Church

This same principle holds true in the Church. Will we stress ethnicity to the point of losing focus on our larger purpose?

We can see from this panoramic view of the world that the challenge is to discover how we in the Church can have true diversity without becoming diverted.

How can we avoid the pitfalls of the world and its fallacious systems of oppression, suppression and concession?

In a time of increasing racial and ethnic tension, the Church must come forth and show the world that we *can* have diversity without diversion. Let's take this wide approach and break it down for application to the Church.

2

The Danger of Overemphasizing Racial Differences

There are three words which need to be addressed with regard to the proper handling of racial differences among God's people. These words are diversity, diversion and divergence.

The first word, *diversity*, is a part of God's creation. It was God's idea, not man's. When understood properly, diversity can be the strength of any endeavor, but if misunderstood it could be the destruction of that endeavor.

To understand the objective of this book, we must begin with working definitions of these words. I see *diversity* as meaning variety, difference, unlikeness or multiple, and *diversion* as the act of turning aside or something that causes a turning aside, such as an amusement, deception or distraction.

One can readily understand by these definitions that the point of this book is to illustrate how overemphasis on differences in race and ethnicity can cause a turning aside from the main goal. We can become amused or fancied by peripheral pursuits to the point that we get off course or off track.

Satan's ultimate goal is for diversion to lead to *divergence*. I see this word *divergence* to mean proceeding from the same point into different directions or receding from each other.

A Principle of Unity

This divergence is the opposite of what Psalm 133:1-3 endorses when it says:

> **Behold, how good and how pleasant it is for brethren to dwell together in unity!**
>
> **It is like the precious ointment upon the head, that ran down upon the beard, even Aaron's beard: that went down to the skirts of his garments;**
>
> **As the dew of Hermon, and as the dew that descended upon the mountains of Zion: for there the Lord commanded the blessing, even life for evermore.**

Notice the psalmist says there is one flow of oil that runs from Aaron's beard down to his feet. It is in this corporate anointing that God has commanded the blessing. Yes, God has decreed that He has blessed unity as a principle. Even when being used for wrong purposes, the principle is still blessed.

Remember the Tower of Babel in Genesis 11. The Lord said in verse 6:

> **Behold, the people is one, and they have all one language; and this they begin to do: and now nothing will be restrained from them, which they have imagined to do.**

This principle of unity is so strong and so powerful that God had to confound their language and scatter them in order to stop them. Otherwise, anything they had wanted to do would have been accomplished.

When Diversity Becomes Diversion

Satan, likewise, understands the power of unity to accomplish good things. It is not surprising then that he would take advantage of racial differences to keep people separated, so that they would be unable to communicate and, if possible, constantly be in strife with each other.

God never intended for differences in color to drive people apart. He intended for the positive characteristics of each race to draw them together. After all, hasn't it always been trade and the mutual benefit of resources and gifts that have brought nations together?

As we discussed earlier, man first seeks his identity, then discovers a cause, submits to a leader and builds a kingdom. One way he realizes his identity is by finding his God-given gift (Romans 12:3-8), then developing it, displaying it and ultimately using it to reach outside of himself to others.

However, when diversity causes us to become proud, thinking more highly of ourselves than we should, we lose the soberness spoken of in Romans 12:3. Our diversity then becomes a diversion — an amusement, a distraction. We become self-deceived into thinking we are more than we really are. This is vanity. Notice the apostle Paul's words from the book of Galatians:

> **For if a man think himself to be something, when he is nothing, he deceiveth himself.**
>
> **But let every man prove his own work, and then shall he have rejoicing in himself alone, and not in another.**
>
> **Galatians 6:3,4**

We will visit these verses again when discussing the relationship between races and our mutual need for one another. However, we are told here that a person who thinks himself to be something when really he is nothing (having no purpose or cause), he deceives himself. If the races feel they are sufficient of themselves, then they are drunk with pride and are deceived.

But by the same token the apostle Paul says that each one should prove his own work, or discover his own value, gifting and identity, that he may rejoice, feel strongly about himself and have good self-esteem. Self-respect is vital to establishing respectable, untainted, unbiased relationships with others.

So one race should not look down upon another because of gifting, relative position or economic status. Neither should another race feel inferior. Feelings of inferiority feed feelings of superiority, so the avoidance of these is crucial to healthy, honest relationships.

Somehow we must learn to see diversity as wealth that belongs to all of us, not a curse that plagues us.

Satan is a deceiver. The prime arena for his deceptions is the arena, not of esteem and self-respect, but of pride. Pride is perverted esteem.

Satan caused the first division ever when he himself was lifted up in pride because of his giftedness. He receded and later seceded from God's kingdom, taking a third of the angels with him (Revelation 12:4-9). It is no great surprise then that he would use such perverted thinking to divide the Church.

I am concerned that many today in the Church are being duped by Satan's clever diversions. He is working against the Church to beguile people away from the simplicity of Christ — His universality and commonality to all. What Satan cannot control and manipulate by oppression, suppression or concession, he dismantles and destroys by secession.

God's Army Must Not Break Ranks!

We must take the Word of God to combat and expose Satan's diversionary tactics and then march as a mighty army into victory. We must **dwell together in unity** (Psalm 133:1), **endeavouring to keep the unity of the Spirit** (the corporate anointing) **in the bond of peace** (Ephesians 4:3). No matter what diversion may come our way, we cannot — and must not — break ranks.

Notice these words about God's army from the prophet Joel:

> The appearance of them is as the appearance of horses; and as horsemen, so shall they run.
>
> Like the noise of chariots on the tops of mountains shall they leap, like the noise of a flame of fire that devoureth the stubble, as a strong people set in battle array.
>
> Before their face the people shall be much pained: all faces shall gather blackness.
>
> They shall run like mighty men; they shall climb the wall like men of war; and they shall march every one on his ways, and they shall not break their ranks:
>
> Neither shall one thrust another; they shall walk every one in his path: and when they fall upon the sword, they shall not be wounded.
>
> They shall run to and fro in the city; they shall run upon the wall, they shall climb up upon the houses; they shall enter in at the windows like a thief.
>
> **Joel 2:4-9**

This great army of the last days is moving together like a band of locusts. It is not breaking ranks or being diverted or receding or being pulled apart.

Oh, that we could understand the blessing of Psalm 133 and the power made available through endeavoring to keep the unity of the Spirit. We can have diversity without diversion. We can be different without being at odds with one another.

Diversion Through Immaturity

Diversity is necessary for the Church to be mature and complete. But, paradoxically, we must be mature in order to handle diversity. If Christ is to have full glory in the Church, we must grow up into Him Who is the Head of all things (Ephesians 4:15).

To become diverted is a sign of immaturity and carnality. It is a lack of understanding of spiritual things.

The apostle Paul describes this immaturity in the book of Ephesians when he says:

> **But unto every one of us is given grace according to the measure of the gift of Christ.**
>
> **That we henceforth be no more children, tossed to and fro, and carried about with every wind of doctrine, by the sleight of men, and cunning craftiness, whereby they lie in wait to deceive.**
>
> **Ephesians 4:7,14**

Notice we are as children when we are led away by every wind of doctrine. This is because children are amused by "new things." A child can be contentedly playing with a toy — let's say a ball — until the parent brings in a toy car. The child throws down the ball and starts playing with the car. New things attract children because little minds are quickly bored and want to be amused. Remember, one of the meanings of diversion is something that causes a turning aside, such as an amusement.

Don't think it strange that Satan would use cunning, crafty, flashy things to draw aside into diversions immature Christians, as well as some mature but discontented ones. As Ephesians 4:14 tells us, men through sleight of hand and the deceitful use of words lie in wait to deceive. Paul says in Second Corinthians 4:2 that ministers should not use the Word of God deceitfully.

Hold to the Simplicity of Christ

This leads us to what may be the most controversial issue of this book. It may challenge some good men and women of God who have great influence in the body of Christ to examine themselves and see whether they be *in the faith.*

Notice I did not use the words, *of the faith,* because they are certainly men and women of God who are called and ordained by God.

But it is rather appropriate to quote from Paul's second letter to the Corinthians:

> **But I fear, lest by any means, as the serpent beguiled Eve through his subtilty, so your minds should be corrupted from the simplicity that is in Christ.**
>
> **2 Corinthians 11:3**

The subtlety of Satan has to do with his ability to use diversions to draw men from the simplicity of Christ. Again, the word *simplicity* means "singleness," "sincerity." It means purity or that from which all else is drawn, fit together, joined or hinged upon.

When we drift away from the centrality and universality of Christ, we run the risk of shipwrecking our faith, no matter how noble our intentions. Let's look now at how easily this can happen.

3
Sound Doctrine vs. Genealogies

There has been a great deal of teaching lately regarding the role of the Black man in the last days. Many prophecies have gone forth in the body of Christ by prominent Charismatic leaders concerning these prophecies. We can see this prophecy coming to pass as Black ministers are rising up to do great exploits for God.

Actually, there have always been Black ministers doing exploits for God; but in a segregated environment and without benefit of modern technology, this has not been widely known. Nevertheless in this hour, ministries headed by Blacks are coming forth in power, excellence, boldness and with great vision.

However, along with this move of God, simultaneous changes have been taking place in our society. An increased interest and emphasis on culture and ethnicity, complicated by a rise in racial strife, has caused a dilemma for Black ministers.

In their communities this increased interest in natural heritage has developed. An extreme faction of the nation of Islam is using an anti-Semitic, anti-Anglo rhetoric to attract many young Blacks. The obvious demand of the Gospel is for these Christian Black ministers to reach out to *all* men, yet many of them have not understood how to deal with this dilemma.

In the attempt to counteract the teaching of the nation of Islam and to meet the rising interest of the community in ethnic and cultural heritage, many have begun to teach on

Blacks in the Bible. While much of the teaching has been very balanced and properly ministered in an edifying manner, some brothers have become extreme in their presentation of this material.

The result for some has been a diversion. They have been distracted from preaching the Gospel and have become preoccupied or overly occupied with natural, carnal things that do not profit.

My emphasis here is on such preoccupation with the natural, carnal realm of life. Not that these aforementioned items — heritage and culture — are not relevant or even important enough to deserve attention and treatment. But to become so overly occupied with them is a diversion which will stop the flow of God's anointing.

Notice the admonition to the Hebrews:

> Be not carried about with divers and strange doctrines. For it is a good thing that the heart be established with grace; not with meats, which have not profited them that have been occupied therein.
>
> **Hebrews 13:9**

Contrast this with the apostle Paul's words to the Ephesians:

> I therefore, the prisoner of the Lord, beseech you that ye walk worthy of the vocation wherewith ye are called,
> With all lowliness and meekness, with longsuffering, forbearing one another in love;
> Endeavouring to keep the unity of the Spirit in the bond of peace.
>
> **Ephesians 4:1-3**

Paul said that our vocation or calling is to endeavor to keep the unity of the Spirit; in other words, to ensure the flow of the anointing.

The word *endeavouring* here is similar to the word *occupied*, which we read in Hebrews 13:9. We are to be occupied with or endeavoring to be transfixed on keeping the unity of the Spirit. We are not to be transfixed on some peripheral or divisive doctrinal pursuit.

Satan fights unity, because unity is necessary in order for the anointing to flow and for the Anointed One to manifest. It is the spirit of antichrist or anti-anointing that subtly comes to divert us and occupy us with fleshly doctrines that do not profit the kingdom of God or build up the body of Christ.

The word *occupy* means literally "to walk or tread about to prove a point."[1] The modern equivalent to the Greek rendering would be people carrying picket signs and marching around a besieged area daily to communicate a message. To prove their point, such people have completely given themselves over to a cause, even to the place of abandoning their normal livelihood.

The tragedy of such endeavors is that in many cases it proves to be unprofitable and divisive and, in some cases, even destructive.

In the body of Christ, a doctrine will occasionally become a cause. People will get carried away with it, transfixed upon it, identified by it and will endeavor to prove it.

Such has become the case for some with regard to the doctrine of genealogies. Many in the Black community of believers have become transfixed on this area to the point of overemphasis and excess. Extremes and excesses will always lead to error.

Truth: The Antidote for Error

The answer or antidote for error is truth — not emotional squabbling and accusations hurled across racial and doctrinal "picket lines" — but truth!

---

[1]Strong, "Greek Dictionary of the New Testament," p. 57, #4043.

According to Ephesians 4:15, **speaking the truth in love** keeps us from being carried away with winds of doctrines and being deceived by Satan's cunning use, or rather his perversion, of the Scriptures and their intended use.

God's way of teaching is described as **...precept upon precept...line upon line; here a little, and there a little** (Isaiah 28:10). This is His method of establishing sound doctrine or truth. If we do not **endure sound doctrine** (2 Timothy 4:3), we **shall be turned unto fables** (v. 4). These *fables* about which we are warned are fabricated, man-made doctrines.

The words *fable* and *fabricate* are derived from the same root word.[2] If there is not enough Scripture to serve as the basis for a doctrine, one must fabricate a supporting doctrine or, at best, slightly bend Scripture to prove a point. Only a determination to pursue a cause or be "carried away" with an idea or concept would cause good men and women to resort to such practices.

We must remember that *for every noble cause there is a noble method of pursuit*. Both the end and the means, if indeed inspired by God, will be mutually righteous and will work together to accomplish the desired results.

There is a world of difference between the aspiration of man and the inspiration of God. Second Timothy 3:16 says:

All scripture is given by inspiration of God, and is profitable for doctrine, for reproof, for correction, for instruction in righteousness.

We can gather from this Scripture that whatever God inspires is profitable. Everything else is vain, fleeting, temporary, passing and not worthy of our focus or the devoting of our faith. To give our time and attention to such is to fall for a diversion.

Our job is to preach the Word of God in season and out of season, regardless of what the present fashion of the

---

[2]Strong, Greek Dictionary, p. 49, #3453.

world may be (2 Timothy 4:2). While an acknowledgment of current affairs is appropriate, *the Gospel* is given that we might be furnished for every good work (2 Timothy 3:17). Jesus is the same yesterday, today and forever (Hebrews 13:8). He is current to meet every need of our world.

First Corinthians 7:31 says, **...the fashion of this world passeth away.** If we grab hold of the fashions of this world rather than holding fast to old, tested, proven, permanent truths of the Word of God, then we will pass away along with the fashion.

How tragic it would be for good, solid ministries, founded on sound biblical truth, to be carried off with a wind of doctrine (Ephesians 4:14) and then pass away. A wind of doctrine is like a vapor that appears but for a moment and then fades away (James 4:14). This speaks of that which is temporal, fleshly or carnal.

How To Stay Sound

Going back to Hebrews 13:9, if we are to be sound in our teaching, there are certain things we are admonished to do. Let's look again at this verse. It says:

Be not carried about with divers and strange doctrines. For it is a good thing that the heart be established with grace....

First, we are not to be "carried away" by taking certain ideas and thoughts too far.

Second, we are to avoid **divers and strange doctrines.** The word *strange* here means "foreign, alien, novel."[3] They are new or untried.

Such doctrines oppose that which is familiar, being taught by ministers we know, and is venerable, tested and proven. In his second epistle to Timothy, the apostle Paul wrote:

---

[3]Strong, Greek Dictionary, p. 50, #3581.

> **But continue thou in the things which thou hast learned and hast been assured of, knowing of whom thou hast learned them.**
>
> **2 Timothy 3:14**

We will remain sound if we continue in that which we have learned, of which we are assured and have proven to work. Similarly, we need to know the person from whom we have learned these truths. We are to stay connected to the spiritual fathers God gave to us.

Thirdly, we must be "established in grace," not the Law. The Law was temporal, a schoolmaster to bring people to Christ (Galatians 3:24). Once Christ came, it was fulfilled in its primary purpose because He was the end of the Law for righteousness. In other words, the Law was to sustain and keep Israel until the Messiah — Christ, the Anointed One — could be born. It was to keep a pure seed and preserve God's promise to Abraham: that through Him (Christ) all the nations (ethnic groups) of the world would be blessed.

No More Purpose for Genealogy

The genealogies were a part of the Law, so they have no purpose now after the birth of Christ. He is universally available and claimable by all nations — not because of the hue of the flesh, but because He is the seed of Abraham, the father of faith (Galatians 3:26-29).

We are of the household, or family, of faith. Once grace came, there was no point in genealogy or law. Christ abolished forever any genealogy's stakes and claims of propriety upon His Person being born of the Spirit and not of the flesh. Not even the Jew can boast of anything under the dispensation of grace. As we have previously discussed, to become preoccupied with such pursuits is not profitable and is contrary to sound doctrine.

We shall discuss in a later chapter the relevance of racial heritage and God's interest in cultural preservation. At this point, it is more important that we speak to those things which have to do with the preservation of and the anointing upon the Church.

Ethnic and racial pride and boasting should be based upon our relationship to Christ, not upon the flesh. Recent emphasis — or should I say overemphasis — on color has brought about a spirit of division in some circles and an increase in carnality.

Spiritual Babies Cannot Receive Sound Doctrine

Let's look at some other words by the apostle Paul to the Corinthian church:

> And I, brethren, could not speak unto you as unto spiritual, but as unto carnal, even as unto babes in Christ.
>
> I have fed you with milk, and not with meat: for hitherto ye were not able to bear it, neither yet now are ye able.
>
> For ye are yet carnal: for whereas there is among you envying, and strife, and divisions, are ye not carnal, and walk as men?
>
> 1 Corinthians 3:1-3

Paul could not give sound doctrine to the Corinthians because they were caught up on winds of doctrines — temporary, carnal beliefs that passed away with the season of fashion. Notice it was because they were acting like spiritual babies.

What Is Sound Doctrine?

This brings us to what God through the prophet Isaiah describes as "sound doctrine":

> Whom shall he teach knowledge? and whom shall he make to understand doctrine? them that are weaned from the milk, and drawn from the breasts.

> For precept must be upon precept, precept upon precept; line upon line, line upon line; here a little, and there a little.
>
> **Isaiah 28:9,10**

Sound doctrine is described in this way:

1. It is not for spiritual babes and the carnally minded. Such cannot endure sound doctrine.

2. It is line upon line, precept upon precept. In other words, sound doctrine is not based upon one isolated Scripture verse or on Scripture that is taken out of context. Being built line upon line and precept upon precept is like building a fortress on a solid foundation. To be *sound* means to be solid or able to withhold and withstand weight, pressure or testing. It can be built upon.

3. It is here a little, and there a little. This means sound doctrine will fit into the overall pattern of Scripture. It will neither conflict nor contradict but will fit into the overall puzzle of the Scriptures without cutting corners or being forced. When we have to cut corners, force it to work or even fabricate doctrine, we are no longer sound; and we are unprofitable.

Avoid the Doctrine of Genealogies

With that in mind, let's look at some of Paul's writings concerning the teaching of genealogies as doctrine. When communicating with Timothy, he said:

> As I besought thee to abide still at Ephesus, when I went into Macedonia, that thou mightest charge some that they teach no other doctrine,
>
> Neither give heed to fables and endless genealogies, which minister questions, rather than godly edifying which is in faith: so do.
>
> Now the end of the commandment is charity out of a pure heart, and of a good conscience, and of faith unfeigned:

From which some having swerved have turned aside unto vain jangling;

Desiring to be teachers of the law; understanding neither what they say, nor whereof they affirm.

1 Timothy 1:3-7

Paul began by emphasizing to Timothy, a bishop, that he was to command the ministers in Ephesus to teach no other doctrine than Christ and Him crucified.

Secondly, he said they were not to give heed, or devote attention, to fables (or fabricated, unsubstantiated doctrine[4]). About such, the apostle Peter said:

For we have not followed cunningly devised fables, when we made known unto you the power and coming of our Lord Jesus Christ, but were eyewitnesses of his majesty.

2 Peter 1:16

In a later chapter Paul said to Timothy:

But refuse profane (or we could say "secular") **and old wives' fables, and exercise thyself rather unto godliness.**

1 Timothy 4:7

We should not teach secular history, science or philosophy as doctrine. In Titus 1:14 Paul exhorts that we are not to give heed or attention to Jewish fables. Again, this is not the calling of a Christian minister.

Genealogies Can Generate Strife

Further in his writing to Titus, Paul warns us not to give heed to endless genealogies, because such discussions generate strife, debates and questions rather than godly edifying. In other words, they can lead to fleshly boasting,

---

[4]This inference is based on Strong's Greek Dictionary, p. 49, #3453 and #3454.

comparisons and divisions rather than edifying the entire body of Christ. He says:

> **This is a faithful saying, and these things I will that thou affirm constantly, that they which have believed in God might be careful to maintain good works. These things are good and profitable unto men.**
>
> **But avoid foolish questions, and genealogies, and contentions, and strivings about the law; for they are unprofitable and vain.**
>
> **Titus 3:8,9**

Unprofitable and vain! This is wood, hay and stubble, and it will receive no reward from the Lord.

The Real Motive for Teaching Genealogies

Some may say, "Well, genealogies are in the Bible, so why shouldn't we teach them?"

Paul is really talking about the purpose and motive of teaching genealogies. If a minister teaches them as a way to point to Christ as Messiah, the Anointed One, then the purpose is just. But if used to build ethnic esteem or self-esteem, they are being used incorrectly.

To build esteem based upon the flesh is fallacious and directly conflicts with God's purpose for the Law, which was to prove all of mankind guilty before Him. All flesh, all ethnic groups, all descendants of Noah's sons — Shem, Ham and Japheth — have had their "day in the sun" to rule the earth. *All* have failed and fallen short of God's glory. The Greeks, Romans, Africans and, yes, even the Israelites, have risen to glory and fallen.

Only the One to Whom Daniel referred as the Ancient of Days (existing eternally before creation) shall rule and reign forever, and His kingdom shall not pass away. (See Daniel 7:9-22.) All nations (ethnic groups) shall declare His glory and worship beneath His throne.

Let's look at the apostle Paul's words in First Corinthians, chapter 1:

> But we preach Christ crucified, unto the Jews a stumblingblock, and unto the Greeks foolishness;
>
> But unto them which are called, both Jews and Greeks, Christ the power of God, and the wisdom of God.
>
> Because the foolishness of God is wiser than men; and the weakness of God is stronger than men.
>
> For ye see your calling, brethren, how that not many wise men after the flesh, not many mighty, not many noble, are called:
>
> But God hath chosen the foolish things of the world to confound the wise; and God hath chosen the weak things of the world to confound the things which are mighty;
>
> And base things of the world, and things which are despised, hath God chosen, yea, and things which are not, to bring to nought things that are:
>
> That no flesh should glory in his presence.
>
> But of him are ye in Christ Jesus, who of God is made unto us wisdom, and righteousness, and sanctification, and redemption:
>
> That, according as it is written, He that glorieth, let him glory in the Lord.
>
> **1 Corinthians 1:23-31**

It says that no flesh — whether white, black, brown, yellow or red — shall glory in His presence. Where is boasting? What purpose is there in esteeming one flesh above another?

Again, notice Paul's teaching in his treatise to the Romans:

> Behold, thou art called a Jew, and restest in the law, and makest thy boast of God.
>
> Thou that makest thy boast of the law, through breaking the law dishonourest thou God?

> For he is not a Jew, which is one outwardly; neither is that circumcision, which is outward in the flesh:
>
> But he is a Jew, which is one inwardly; and circumcision is that of the heart, in the spirit, and not in the letter; whose praise is not of men, but of God.
>
> What advantage then hath the Jew? or what profit is there of circumcision?
>
> Much every way: chiefly, because that unto them were committed the oracles of God.
>
> Where is boasting then? It is excluded. By what law? of works? Nay: but by the law of faith.
>
> Romans 2:17,23,28,29; 3:1,2,27

Paul carefully and precisely expelled the idea that any ethnic group — including the Israelites — could boast of anything in the flesh. In fact, he said that if there was any advantage, it was in the realization that the Jews had the Word committed to them. Not that their skin was a certain hue, but that they had received the oracles of God. Why? Because faith comes by hearing the Word (Romans 10:17).

Boasting comes by the law of faith (Romans 3:27). Faith connects us to Christ. Christ connects us to Abraham as the original Jew. In Galatians 3:29 the apostle Paul says, **If ye be Christ's, then are ye Abraham's seed**. He had said in Romans 2:28,29 that a Jew is not by outward flesh but by that which is within. Faith is in the heart! God said that through Abraham's seed all the nations of the earth would be blessed (Galatians 3:8).

So, as God sees it, there are only two races of people: believers and unbelievers.

To get bogged down into discussions of genealogies and races is fruitless and pointless. Not that God has done away with the nations, but for the purposes of the Gospel and righteousness, the teaching of genealogies is fruitless.

In fact, genealogies are not listed in the Bible so that we can trace races or ethnic groups, but to point us to the birth of Jesus. God's family is made up of all racial groups; it is, according to First Peter 2:9, an *ethnos* — a holy nation. The rest is history and of no eternal value.

There Is No Division in Christ Jesus

Now let's look again in First Timothy, chapter 1. It says:

> **Now the end** (goal or purpose) **of the commandment** (the Law) **is charity out of a pure heart, and of a good conscience, and of faith unfeigned:**
>
> **From which some having swerved have turned aside** (been diverted) **unto vain jangling.**
>
> 1 Timothy 1:5,6

Notice that the end, or goal, of the Law was love, hope and faith — not fruitless discussions and strivings over outward and fleshly things.

I believe Paul was referencing to some trilogy in this verse as was mentioned in First Corinthians 13:13 when he said, **And now abideth faith, hope, charity, these three....** I believe that good conscience and hope are basically interchangeable as they both speak of confidence, boldness and positive, favorable expectation. Paul said these three abide forever. But debates and strivings over outward and fleshly things are fruitless in terms of eternal value.

Galatians 5:6 says:

> **For in Jesus Christ neither circumcision availeth any thing, nor uncircumcision; but faith which worketh by love.**

In Christ — the Anointing and the Anointed One — there is no distinction of color or ethnicity. Christ both encompasses and transcends all barriers of the flesh. He tore down the middle wall of partition that had separated Jew from Gentile, thus every other racial and ethnic barrier has been abolished (Ephesians 2:14).

Don't Be Diverted!

But Galatians 5:7 says:

> **Ye did run well; who did hinder you that ye should not obey the truth?**

The word *hinder* here means to confuse, disorient or lead off track; in other words, to cause a diversion.[5] We cannot allow diversity to lead to diversion. Satan wants to divert us from the plans and purposes of God.

So the apostle Paul says in First Timothy 1:6 that if we get away from the true purpose of the Law, which includes genealogies, we run the risk of swerving or being **turned aside** (diverted) **unto vain jangling**.

Taylor's translation says, **But these teachers have missed the whole idea.**[6]

The Amplified Bible renders the second half of First Timothy 1:6 as having **wandered away into vain arguments and discussions and purposeless talk.**

In First Timothy 6:20 and Second Timothy 2:16, Timothy, as well as all believers, is advised to avoid vain babblings. The word *babbling* in its most crude sense means collecting scraps, leftovers, refuse or garbage.[7] It has the connotation of taking from a junk pile or garbage heap something that has been discarded and is spoiled, antiquated or obsolete.

---

[5]Based on definition of "hinder" in *Expository Dictionary of New Testament Words* by W. E. Vine, (Old Tappan: Revell, 1940), Vol. II, p. 221: "lit. to cut into, was used of impeding persons by breaking up the road, or by placing an obstacle sharply in the path; hence, metaphorically, . . . of hindering progress in the Christian life, Galatians 5:7, where the significance virtually is 'who broke up the road along which you were travelling so well?' . . . ."

[6]Vaughn Curtis, *The Word, The Bible From 26 Translations.* (Moss Point, MS: Mathis Publisher, 1988), p. 2419.

[7]According to *Expository Dictionary of New Testament Words* by W. E. Vine, (Old Tappan: Revell, 1940), Vol. I, p. 93, "babbler . . . seems to have been used of a man accustomed to hang about the streets and markets, picking up scraps which fall from loads; hence a parasite, who lives at the expense of others, a hanger on."

Paul said we should not resort to picking up scraps and being garbage collectors of the outdated Law. We should be feasting from the table of grace. In other words, why keep bringing up "dead issues" which have been dealt with through the New Covenant? We are not vain babblers but Gospel preachers. There is no need to beat a dead horse; he isn't going to run!

We can harp on something until we are utterly exhausted, but it won't change the meaning, intent or purpose. If we misunderstand or don't apply the Word of God properly, we won't get results. This is what Paul was asserting when he said:

> **Desiring to be teachers of the law; understanding neither what they say, nor whereof they affirm.**
>
> **1 Timothy 1:7**

To affirm means "to confirm thoroughly (by words)," "affirm constantly."[8] It means to be constantly teaching, propagating or harping on something.

God does not want us to take on teachings of genealogies and racial superiority as a vocation. That which we constantly affirm, we will propagate. We should be careful not to propagate anything that might lead to division or magnify differences.

Stay With Sound Doctrine!

God has worked progressively throughout His Word to eliminate distinctions in the realm of the Spirit. For us to go backwards to a system of separation and emphasis upon the flesh would be counter-productive. In fact, it would be anti-Christ or anti-anointing. As stated earlier, anything that stops the flow of the anointing or hinders the unity needed for the corporate anointing is anti-anointing.

---

[8]Strong, Greek Dictionary, p. 22, #1226.

Let us therefore make a decision to stay with sound doctrine. We have a wonderful treatise in the letters of the apostle Paul, inspired by the Holy Spirit, pleading with us to avoid the pitfalls of diversionary doctrines.

Diversion may ultimately lead to subversion. One Greek word for *subverting* is *katastrŏphé;*[9] in English, *catastrophe*. Teaching the doctrine of genealogy, with overemphasis on skin color, could have catastrophic results upon the faith of some believers.

Again, notice some of Paul's words to Timothy:

Of these things put them in remembrance, charging them before the Lord that they strive not about words to no profit, but to the subverting of the hearers.
2 Timothy 2:14

Not only is fleshly oriented teaching unprofitable, it can in fact subvert (shipwreck or overthrow) the faith of some.

Those who are not overthrown may be subverted to a lesser degree. The word *subverting* as used in Acts 15:24 means "to upset";[10] it means to be disturbing or unsettling. It has the connotation of scattering everything that has been gathered, with the workman then having to start all over again, redoing what had previously been done.

I have personally ministered to people who were recovering from such unsettling experiences. These people once were operating in the principles of faith, beginning in the Spirit, but were trying to be perfected in the flesh. To see them struggling with their identity was indeed frustrating. Then I understood the compassion of Paul when he said to the Galatians:

This only would I learn of you, Received ye the Spirit by the works of the law, or by the hearing of faith?

[9]Strong, Greek Dictionary, p. 41, #2692.
[10]Strong, Greek Dictionary, p. 11, #384.

Are ye so foolish? having begun in the Spirit, are ye now made perfect by the flesh?

Have ye suffered so many things in vain? if it be yet in vain.

He therefore that ministereth to you the Spirit, and worketh miracles among you, doeth he it by the works of the law, or by the hearing of faith?

Even as Abraham believed God, and it was accounted to him for righteousness.

Know ye therefore that they which are of faith, the same are the children of Abraham.

Galatians 3:2-7

Hold to the Basics of Faith

To see how this applies to you, ask yourself a few questions:

Did you receive the Holy Spirit by tracing your genealogy and by knowing how many people of color are in the Bible?

Having been born again from above, are you going to be perfected by earthly ancestry?

Have you identified with the crucified Christ and suffered in the flesh in vain?

Does that crucified flesh now have occasion to glory?

Does the person who is ministering the New Covenant to you and is working miracles among you, do it because he or she is White, Black, Jewish or of any other race?

Was Abraham made righteous because he was a Jew, or because he believed God?

Are we the children of Abraham because we are his direct descendants, or because we believe in his God?

Oh, foolish Christians, are we so shallow, so carnal that we are so easily distracted?

These words may seem harsh. Some may say, "Just who does he think he is, talking to me like that?"

As Paul told Timothy:

> **If thou put the brethren in remembrance of these things, thou shalt be a good minister of Jesus Christ, nourished up in the words of faith and of good doctrine, whereunto thou hast attained.**
>
> **1 Timothy 4:6**

Good ministers are required of God to put their brothers and sisters in remembrance of the basics of faith. These basics are the things we tend to let slip, because they are foundational (Hebrews 2:1).

Nobody goes around raving about the foundations of great edifices, like the Empire State Building or the Sears Tower. Those foundations are unseen, thus they are taken for granted.

We tend to allow the basics to slip. But we must take heed to ourselves and to the doctrine, continuing in them; for in doing this, we shall save both ourselves and those who hear us (1 Timothy 4:16).

It is easy to be diverted, to get off track. If we are not careful, what started out as a side trip could become a destination. We must be mature enough to appreciate our diversity without being diverted.

Let us endeavor to be ministers of Jesus Christ. The members of our congregations may be of different hues and ethnic backgrounds, but our message is still the same: Jesus Christ and Him crucified (1 Corinthians 2:2).

That leads us to the next Scripture found in this discourse. Is there a proper use of the Law, and can reference to heritage and ethnicity have a place in the Church? Let's find out.

4

Lawful Use of the Law

But we know that the law is good, if a man use it lawfully.

1 Timothy 1:8

As mentioned in the introduction, we are living in a world that is becoming increasingly more ethnically minded. People are searching for identity even as we embark into the twenty-first century, which is bringing with it a global economy, free trade and international corporations. Paradoxically, the geographical borders of nations are being erased, while ethnic borders within are becoming more evident.

Overcoming cultural, ethnic and religious barriers has always been a challenge for the Church and continues, even today, to pose enormous obstacles. How do we preach Christ to people who are biased? How do we share truth with those who are steeped in philosophy, cultural mores or various taboos that distort or hinder the presentation of Christ?

Knowing that these challenges would be before us, God has given to Christians certain liberties which facilitate the crossing of cultural barriers to present the Gospel.

As First Corinthians 10:23 says:

All things are lawful for me, but all things are not expedient: all things are lawful for me, but all things edify not.

We are permitted to use the Law and methodology associated with it as long as it is expedient to the cause of

Christ and edifies — not divides — the body of Christ. In other words, any deviation or compromise we make in deference to the Law must ultimately be eliminated for the good of the Gospel and for the glory of God. The apostle Paul put it this way:

> For though I be free from all men, yet have I made myself servant unto all, that I might gain the more.
>
> And unto the Jews I became as a Jew, that I might gain the Jews; to them that are under the law, as under the law, that I might gain them that are under the law;
>
> To them that are without law, as without law, (being not without law to God, but under the law to Christ,) that I might gain them that are without law.
>
> To the weak became I as weak, that I might gain the weak: I am made all things to all men, that I might by all means save some.
>
> And this I do for the gospel's sake, that I might be partaker thereof with you.
>
> **1 Corinthians 9:19-23**

We then, as Paul, must do all we can to win people to Christ.

To have the privilege of ministering to the Jews, Paul observed their traditions, even though their traditions were vain. He had his head shaved and Timothy circumcised (Acts 18:18; 16:3).

Paul's vow was referred to as a vow of separation or a Nazarite vow (Numbers 6:2-21). It essentially involved abstinence from wine and strong drink, as well as following a strict diet (Numbers 6:3,4). The Nazarites were not allowed to cut their hair until the time of separation was complete, at which time the person taking the vow would appear before the priest, shave his head and offer the hair as part of the peace offering sacrifice (Numbers 6:18,19).

This purification ritual was completed by the apostle Paul in order to placate James and the apostles, as well as other Jews who accused Paul of teaching Gentiles to disregard the Law of Moses (Acts 21:21-26), for even many of the believing Jews continued in the observance of the Law.

Paul, knowing full well that Christ's sacrifice was sufficient for him, condescended to this Jewish tradition in order to reach his brethren. This is the Paul who was so zealous for his people that he said in Romans 9:3, **For I could wish that myself were accursed from Christ for my brethren, my kinsmen according to the flesh.** What zeal he had for his natural brethren, pushing the very limits in order to reach them. And imagine Timothy as an adult being circumcised in order to be received of the Jews!

Likewise to reach the Gentiles, Paul ate foods that were foreign to his Jewish upbringing and adjusted himself to their culture.

Notice in First Corinthians 10:26,27 that Paul instructs the church in Corinth: **For the earth is the Lord's, and the fulness thereof. If any of them that believe not bid you to a feast, and ye be disposed to go; whatsoever is set before you, eat, asking no question for conscience sake.**

Likewise, he instructed Timothy: **For every creature of God is good, and nothing to be refused, if it be received with thanksgiving: For it is sanctified by the word of God and prayer** (1 Timothy 4:4,5).

It can be logically inferred by Paul's instruction to others that he adapted himself to the culture and diet of the people to whom he preached the Gospel.

Whether dealing with either Jew or Gentile, Paul strove lawfully, following the rules of expedience and edification.

We Must Be Wise!

Similarly, situations and trends in our culture may cause us to adapt our methods in order to reach people. But we must use wisdom to win them rather than alienate them. Proverbs 11:30 says that **...he that winneth souls is wise.**

Paul said concerning the church at Corinth:

> **...being crafty** (or we could say "wise"), **I caught you with guile** (or "bait"[1] — lure or disguise).
>
> **2 Corinthians 12:16**

Sometimes the only blessing people can receive is one in disguise. Becoming all things to all men (people) is lawful in Christ because He abolished all barriers to access. But failure to point them to Christ as their Righteousness is compromise.

Such things as fleshly disguises are not for Christians but for those who are lost and have no understanding of sound doctrine. Once people are saved, they can be taught about Christ as their Wisdom, Righteousness, Sanctification and Redemption (1 Corinthians 1:30).

The Only Reason
for Ethnically Based Teaching

Having this foundational understanding, it is lawful then, for only one reason, that Christian ministers be allowed to make references to items of ethnic content: to refute certain claims being made by radical Black religious groups. The Bible is proclaimed by them to be the "White man's book" and Jesus to be the "White man's Savior." Through such fallacious doctrines as these, Black Muslims have been working and are continuing to work at recruiting large numbers of young Black males.

The ethnic references of the Bible may appeal to the carnal mind of oppressed, dispossessed Blacks, under siege

---

[1]Strong, Greek Dictionary, p. 24, #1388.

by radical, often racist and militant, religious and social groups. In this case, it is acceptable to be used as an evangelistic tool.

To the extent that Black leaders have to deal with issues unique to the Black experience and social status, ethnically directed teaching may be necessary.

Only God knows the motives and intent of a person's heart which lead to his actions. Each time we take liberty in the Word of God, we must ensure that it is expedient for the cause of Christ and that it will edify the body of Christ.

Quite often in a racially mixed congregation, it is necessary to address ethnocentric issues. We cannot feel uncomfortable doing this — it is a reality!

Just Don't Compromise the Gospel

We should be cautioned, however, that the Gospel is not a social movement or a tool for social revolution. The Bible's references to ethnicity are not designed to build self-esteem but rather to ensure all people that God is not a respecter of persons (Acts 10:34). He does not esteem flesh, but that which is in a person's heart (1 Samuel 16:7).

It is evident from Scripture that we all are equal in God's sight; one race should not esteem itself greater than another. Even we as Christians are debtors to the heathen, bound and constrained by the love of God to spend our lives in an effort to reconcile the lost (Romans 1:13-19; 5:8-12).

We must be cautious of a "liberation theology" which concentrates more on the social and external than on the individual and internal. The use of religion as a cloak to promote political and social ends, and even the overthrow of authority, has been used quite extensively in third-world nations. Liberation theology views Jesus as a rebel Who went about setting people free by the elimination of social and governmental injustices. Jesus never taught or endorsed the overthrow of governments, class-warfare resistance techniques or any of the aforementioned things.

If we compromise the Gospel by twisting it to fit our social or racial agendas, the result will be that our faith is shipwrecked.

Man's esteem problems are based on alienation from God, His acceptance and approval. We all like to have the acceptance and approval of others, but we are foolish if we allow our self-esteem to hinge upon it.

Our message should be: "Through Christ, you can do all things. Not because you are Black and have Christ (or White and have Christ). But because you can do all things through Christ, the Anointed One, Who strengthens you" (Philippians 4:13).

Be Careful Not To Answer Error With More Error

We must be sure that we are not preaching out of contention, envy and strife. As Paul wrote:

> **Some indeed preach Christ even of envy and strife; and some also of good will:**
>
> **The one preach Christ of contention, not sincerely, supposing to add affliction to my bonds:**
>
> **But the other of love, knowing that I am set for the defence of the gospel.**
>
> **Philippians 1:15-17**

While there remains a great deal of prejudice and even racism within the body of Christ, we must be careful not to answer error with more error. Many Blacks who have been offended by acts of racial prejudice have become embittered. That bitterness exaggerates their message and agitates the hearers.

In a later chapter, we will address some of the concerns of Black leaders in the body of Christ regarding prejudice and racism. But at this point let's simply say that two wrongs don't make a right. Answering prejudice, racism and separation with more prejudice, racism and separation is not the answer; it will only compound the offense.

Contention Opens the Floodgates

The book of Proverbs states:

The beginning of strife is as when one letteth out water: therefore leave off contention, before it be meddled with.

Proverbs 17:14

As we read in Philippians, the apostle Paul knew the danger of preaching the Gospel out of contention. The beginning of strife is like a small leak in a dam; but when that strife turns to contention, it is like opening the floodgates. In other words, strife, which is inspired by the devil, can be remedied and the dam repaired unless someone meddles with that strife. Racial strife is always stirred up by those who become contentious.

Contention — the Result of Pride

Notice these words from another proverb concerning contention:

Only by pride cometh contention: but with the well advised is wisdom.

Proverbs 13:10

Contention is a result of pride. In fact, this verse lets us know that it comes *only* by pride. Racial strife always has a little trickle flowing, reminding us of its potent force for hatred, violence and destruction. Only when prideful men and women on either side meddle with it will the dam be broken.

Pride is the original sin committed by Lucifer. It came about as a result of perverted self-esteem. God created Lucifer more beautiful than all the angels and gave him a high position. But he was corrupted by his beauty and lifted up in pride (Isaiah 14:12-15).

That's what pride is: perverted self-esteem.

Pride brings with it an attitude of haughtiness or rebellion. Rebellion brings with it strife. Strife turns to contention. Contention leads to sedition. Sedition causes followers to choose sides, which brings about division.

To aid you in understanding this progression, let's briefly define these words. *Pride* is excessive self-esteem or conceit. Romans 12:3 says we are not to think of ourselves more highly than we ought. *Haughtiness* is defined as being arrogantly proud. *Arrogance* leads to rebellion; we could define *arrogance* as open defiance toward an authority or convention. *Strife* is discord or conflict. *Contention,* on the other hand, is controversy, rivalry or competition. It is pulling action to the underlying condition. *Sedition* is behavior or language which incites others to rebel against established government or authority. The end result again is *division* or separation into factions.

One-third of the angels followed Lucifer in his contention with God (Revelation 12:4). As a result, the war continues even to this day. Little wonder then that Satan lurks behind racism. Pride (or prideful attitudes) is just waiting for an opportunity to spurn contention among the leaders. Satan wants to take self-esteem and God-given self-respect and pervert it into pride so as to bring about contention. He wants the Gospel to be preached out of contention.

Wisdom Is Better Than Contention

As the second part of Proverbs 13:10 says: **...but with the well advised is wisdom.**

The key to avoiding prideful contentions is to be well advised. Wisdom is better than war. We can be wise or we can be foolish. Proverbs 18:6 says:

A fool's lips enter into contention, and his mouth calleth for strokes.

We can have good, frank, well-advised discussions on controversial subjects without becoming contentious. But if we are ill-advised and go off half-cocked, we will stir up strife and contention. We cannot afford to have foolish, hot-headed, unbalanced people leading discussions about controversial issues. We can see the ill effects of this in our national government, and it works the same way in the Church.

Wisdom is better than contention. Proverbs 22:10 says:

Cast out the scorner (he who refuses wisdom), **and contention shall go out; yea, strife and reproach shall cease.**

We should avoid or cast away divisive, unbalanced, ill-advised teachings and writings generated by persons who are contentious. When we do so, contention, strife and the reproach of it shall cease. In other words, we don't have to choose sides when contention comes. This only feeds the pride that is behind contention.

Have you ever noticed that when something controversial comes along people start taking their own opinion polls?

What do you think of Brother So-and-so's book?

What do you think about the So-and-so movement?

Brother So-and-so and Brother So-and-so are at odds. Whose side are you on?

We can stop this force of contention in its tracks if we will use the wisdom of God.

When controversy comes, people often get upset with me because I won't declare whose side I am on. They say, "Let's confront Brother So-and-so," or "Let's straighten out this thing or that thing." What they really want to do is to contend — not confront.

But notice the wisdom in the Word of God:

> **He that hath knowledge spareth his words** (or waits until the right time)**: and a man of understanding is of an excellent spirit.**
>
> . **Even a fool, when he holdeth his peace, is counted wise: and he that shutteth his lips is esteemed a man of understanding.**
>
> **Proverbs 17:27,28**

Confronting an issue at the wrong time and in the wrong way will only lead to more contention. Wise, seasoned leaders know how to defuse a bomb; the foolish will only set it off.

Beware of contentious people who have an "ax to grind" or a "chip on their shoulder." Oftentimes a root of bitterness has entered a person or offense has taken hold of him. Proverbs 18:19 says:

> **A brother offended is harder to be won than a strong city: and their contentions are like the bars of a castle.**

Later, we will discuss some of the things over which brothers are offended and we will look at some of the causes of offense. As Hebrews 12:15 says, many can be defiled by a root of bitterness if it is not resolved. Bitter contentions and the subsequent divisions caused by them could greatly hinder the anointing of God in a revival and curtail the outpouring of the Holy Spirit.

Contend for the Faith!

That is why we must make up our minds, like the apostle Paul, to contend for only one thing — the faith. In Philippians 1:17 he says:

> **...knowing that I am set for the defence of the gospel.**

This book is being written, not to defend one camp or straighten out another, but in defense of the Gospel.

As Jude said, we are to **...earnestly contend for the faith which was once delivered unto the saints** (v. 3). In this same verse he referred to **the faith** as **the common salvation**.

Christ is not divided. He does not have separate salvation plans for Whites, Blacks, Hispanics and other groups. While there may be many causes and purposes in a diverse world, we must only contend for the faith. Nothing else is worthy of contention.

We should not, however, be contending for the faith of various denominations. Neither should we contend in areas involving race or ethnicity. As Ephesians 4:4 says:

> **There is one body, and one Spirit, even as ye are called in one hope of your calling.**

For this we must contend!

The Ministry of Reconciliation

A good and frank discussion of issues and the resolution of grievances is good and proper. This has always been God's way. We are not suggesting that contending for the faith means ignoring legitimate grievances and causes. Proverbs 18:18 says:

> **The lot causeth contentions to cease, and parteth between the mighty.**

God expects leaders, especially those with great influence, to come together and resolve areas that have become matters of contention. This happened when racial strife broke out in the Church. (See Acts 6 and 15.)

We must not allow differences to lead to diversions from "the faith." We must not become involved in "choosing sides" when contentions arise. When controversy comes, we should be slow to speak, choosing the time and words that make for peace and reconciliation.

Our ministry is reconciliation (2 Corinthians 5:19). This reconciliation cannot be brought about through the study of genealogies nor by merely placating grievances through laws and decrees. God is precise in His Word about reconciliation and what it means.

Without an understanding of true biblical reconciliation, we will be struggling with the racial issue for years down the road. Let us look now into this great central theme of God's Word: reconciliation.

5
Reconciliation — The Great Truth

> I exhort therefore, that, first of all, supplications, prayers, intercessions, and giving of thanks, be made for all men;
>
> For kings, and for all that are in authority; that we may lead a quiet and peaceable life in all godliness and honesty.
>
> For this is good and acceptable in the sight of God our Saviour;
>
> Who will have all men to be saved, and to come unto the knowledge of the truth.
>
> For there is one God, and one mediator between God and men, the man Christ Jesus;
>
> Who gave himself a ransom for all, to be testified in due time.
>
> Whereunto I am ordained a preacher, and an apostle, (I speak the truth in Christ, and lie not;) a teacher of the Gentiles in faith and verity.
>
> 1 Timothy 2:1-7

This passage of Scripture conveys the key to peace and reconciliation of all nations and peoples of the earth. It is a truth which is so mighty and powerful that if the world had a revelation of it, it would immediately bring peace and goodwill to earth.

One Mediator Between God and Men

There is one central truth that Satan has kept hidden from man over the centuries. It is found in verse 5. Again, it says:

For there is one God, and one mediator between God and men, the man Christ Jesus.

Notice that, preceding this, verse 4 says of God our Savior that He:

...will have all men to be saved, and to come unto the knowledge of the truth.

Let me again emphasize this one great truth: **there is one God, and one mediator between God and men, the man Christ Jesus.** It is God's will for men to be reconciled to Him and to each other, but it can only happen through His anointed Mediator, Christ Jesus.

Man Must Be Reconciled to Man

We have placed a great deal of emphasis, and rightly so, on reconciling man to God. But that is only half of God's will. He wants us to be reconciled to each other. Notice this passage does not say there is only one mediator between God and *man,* but between God and *men* — plural. This denotes all nations, all diverse ethnic groups.

To understand the significance of this revelation, we must first understand the Bible definition of reconciliation. *Reconcile* means "to change mutually," "exchange."[1]

When the root meanings of all the words are combined, reconciliation means to bring back, to adjust. "To change mutually" indicates making different in order to make the same.

Summarily, reconciliation is the process of comparing differences, making adjustments, bringing differences into balance, and making things right or justifying the differences. *Justifying* in this sense refers to restitution or making up for the difference. Christ makes up the difference

---

[1]Strong, Greek Dictionary, p. 40, #2643 and #2644.

between God's standard of righteousness and our own righteousness. Likewise, true reconciliation would involve "making right" any injustice or inequity which may exist with regard to the races. This process is so thorough that there is no evidence or trace of any difference having ever existed.

When a husband and wife have reconciled after a separation, if true reconciliation takes place, there is no evidence of that separation. There is no one-upmanship, no getting even, no grudges, no bringing up of the past.

We have made only token progress in race relations over the past years, because we have not even attempted reconciliation. We have tended to placate rather than reconciliate.

Placating or appeasing one another is a gracious act, but *reconciliation* is a transaction that changes, not just the feelings, but the state or status. It is the transaction that makes compatible and as one with each other those who were formerly different, or even in opposition.

True Reconciliation *Must* Come

True reconciliation will accomplish the following:

1. Remove all past differences that caused alienation.

2. Remove any barriers or distinctions that would cause separation.

3. Restore any rights or privileges necessary for affirmation.

This was done through the Anointed Christ. No One but Christ Jesus is capable or worthy of holding this place. He is the one and only Mediator between God and man.

People who cause separation and division, whether knowingly or unknowingly, are creating the position of mediator. If such leaders are not conciliatory in their message and demeanor, they will, in fact, hinder the cause of Christ.

Leaders of different racial groups may continue to hold on to the past in fear, ignorance and unforgiveness. If so, they will cause their followers to be alienated from other racial groups, and those followers, in turn, will alienate others.

Those who continue allowing barriers, such as skin color and culture, to cause separation and division will be hindering the anointing of Christ. Reconciliation, on the other hand, includes restoration of rights and privileges that are hindering equality between racial groups. It puts everyone on an equal standing. Christ is the only One uniquely qualified to serve as Mediator. Let's see why.

By necessity, a mediator must be one who is taken from among and can fairly represent all parties. Christ can mediate between God and man because He is both God and man. He can represent heaven and earth because He came from both places. He can represent all men because He came from all men. He is called the Son of Man.

When examining Jesus' earthly genealogy, we can see that each of the three major ethnic classes — Shem, Ham and Japheth — are included in His genealogy. So Christ alone can forgive anything between God and men.

Being the Son of Man, He can demand forgiveness and settle disputes among the races and ethnic groups.

Being the seed of Abraham, the father of our faith, He can confer heirship upon all people, giving full equality, privilege and right to all who are His (Galatians 3:29).

If all people knew and understood this great and universal truth, all strife among races and nations would cease. Christ is the Mediator of the New Covenant, based upon better promises (Hebrews 8:6). Through Him, all can come to God and to each other.

Let's look closer at what God has done to reconcile the races.

The Process of Reconciliation

In the beginning, Adam became the "federal head" of all creation. All races or ethnic groups came out of his blood. The apostle Paul said this when addressing the Athenians:

> **And He made from one [common origin, one source, one blood] all nations of men to settle on the face of the earth....**
>
> **Acts 17:26 AMP**

All ethnic groups came from one blood: the blood of Adam. When Adam fell, all of mankind fell with him. Therefore, man's greatest need was redemption, or reconciliation back to God.

In Genesis, chapter 6, we see how man became more wicked, causing God to cut back on the length of their days. But when sin continued its rampage, God decided to judge the earth, ultimately purging all mankind, except for Noah and his family.

After the Flood, Noah's family was commanded to replenish the earth, namely through his three sons: Shem, Ham and Japheth. Genesis, chapter 10, gives the complete genealogy of the sons of Noah.[2] Shem headed up the Shemites — the Jews, Arabs and Orientals. Ham fathered the Hamitic people, primarily the Africans. Japheth produced the White, or European, people. Though there were three primary races or ethnic groups, they were still of one blood — the blood of Adam through Noah.

Then in Genesis, chapter 11, we see that humanism had begun to take hold. Instead of man seeking God, he began to make himself as god with his own system of worship.

---

[2]Finis J. Dake. *Annotated Reference Bible.* (Lawrenceville, GA: Dake's Bible Sales, 1963), p. 40.

Although there were three major ethnic groups, they intermingled together and all had the same language. Because they did not seek God, He confounded their speech, giving them distinct and diverse dialects, and scattered them over the face of the earth (Genesis 11:1-9).

It is at this time that many theologians believe the landmass was divided, with continents and islands coming into being.[3] This is likely being referred to by the apostle Paul in this portion of Scripture:

> ...and (God) **hath determined the times before appointed, and the bounds of their habitation;**
> **That they should seek the Lord, if haply they might feel after him, and find him, though he be not far from every one of us.**
>
> **Acts 17:26,27**

Deuteronomy 32:8 says likewise:

> **When the Most High divided to the nations their inheritance, when he separated the sons of Adam, he set the bounds of the people according to the number of the children of Israel.**

Because of man's idolatry and humanistic thought, it was originally God's idea to separate the nations or ethnic groups in order that they might seek Him. Specifically, He was looking toward Israel as a people to serve Him, but generally He took the action of separation so that all nations would seek Him first.

Why is this so effective?

First, when man is in solitude, he begins to be introspective, and with introspection comes discovery of weaknesses and inadequacies. This discovery causes man to seek God.

Secondly, solitude or isolation eliminates distractions, giving man full opportunity to seek God.

---

[3]Dake, p. 10, note f.

Thirdly, solitude brings dependency within the group or culture, strengthening that culture and its belief system, its morals and its values. Too much dependence upon outside sources hinders dependence upon God.

So God established "bounds of habitation" for nations so that man would put his vertical relationship with God before his horizontal relationships with man. But it is clear that God was not advocating separation of the races as a divine principle or goal.

Through Jesus, There Is No More Need for Separation

Once a pure seed was secured through the seed of Abraham with the birth of Christ, there was no longer any need for separation. As we will see from John's gospel, the Lord Jesus' discourse to the woman at the well brings home this point.

> Then cometh he to a city of Samaria, which is called Sychar, near to the parcel of ground that Jacob gave to his son Joseph.
>
> Now Jacob's well was there. Jesus therefore, being wearied with his journey, sat thus on the well: and it was about the sixth hour.
>
> There cometh a woman of Samaria to draw water: Jesus saith unto her, Give me to drink.
>
> (For his disciples were gone away unto the city to buy meat.)
>
> Then saith the woman of Samaria unto him, How is it that thou, being a Jew, askest drink of me, which am a woman of Samaria? for the Jews have no dealings with the Samaritans.
>
> **John 4:5-9**

Because of the years of strict separation demanded by the Law in order to preserve the lineage of Abraham, Isaac and Jacob, the Jews were very prejudiced toward other races. In fact, they considered non-Jews to be "dogs" since they were not partakers of the covenant.

This is why the Samaritan woman was shocked when Jesus asked her for a drink of water. As she said in verse 9, the Jews had no dealings with the Samaritans.

Then later in this chapter, Jesus reveals that the prohibition of separate worship had come to an end and the method of fellowshipping with and worshipping God had changed. Let's continue with their conversation:

> **Jesus saith unto her, Woman, believe me, the hour cometh, when ye shall neither in this mountain, nor yet at Jerusalem, worship the Father.**
>
> **Ye worship ye know not what: we know what we worship; for salvation is of the Jews.**
>
> **But the hour cometh, and now is, when the true worshippers shall worship the Father in spirit and in truth: for the Father seeketh such to worship him.**
>
> **God is a Spirit: and they that worship him must worship him in spirit and in truth.**
>
> **John 4:21-24**

Jesus announces a new circumcision, a new way of identifying God's people that transcended racial lines. He declared, **God is a Spirit: and they that worship him must worship him in spirit and in truth** (v. 24).

With the promised Seed in the earth, there was no longer a need to establish "bounds of habitation." God wanted all people to know the Messiah and to worship Him.

Even during the time of separation, God never allowed Israel to mistreat or look down on those whom the Mosaic Law referred to as "strangers." It was separation but not racism. Exodus 22:21 says:

> **Thou shalt neither vex a stranger, nor oppress him: for ye were strangers in the land of Egypt.**

God allowed the mixed multitude from out of Egypt to worship with the Israelites, but a wall of partition was placed between the Jews and the "strangers" (Ephesians 2:14).

There Is Peace Between the Races in Christ Jesus

Notice the apostle Paul's words in Ephesians, chapter 2, about the work Christ did:

> Wherefore remember, that ye being in time past Gentiles in the flesh, who are called Uncircumcision by that which is called the Circumcision in the flesh made by hands;
>
> That at that time ye were without Christ, being aliens from the commonwealth of Israel, and strangers from the covenants of promise, having no hope, and without God in the world:
>
> But now in Christ Jesus ye who sometimes were far off are made nigh by the blood of Christ.
>
> For he is our peace, who hath made both one, and hath broken down the middle wall of partition between us;
>
> Having abolished in his flesh the enmity, even the law of commandments contained in ordinances; for to make in himself of twain one new man, so making peace;
>
> And that he might reconcile both unto God in one body by the cross, having slain the enmity thereby:
>
> And came and preached peace to you which were afar off, and to them that were nigh.
>
> For through him we both have access by one Spirit unto the Father.
>
> Now therefore ye are no more strangers and foreigners, but fellowcitizens with the saints, and of the household of God.
>
> **Ephesians 2:11-19**

In the flesh before the advent of Christ, all non-Jews were aliens and strangers to the commonwealth of Israel, and to the covenants and promises. But as verse 13 says, we have been brought nigh by the blood of Christ.

Verse 14 says He is our peace, having made both Jew and Gentile as one, and He has broken down the middle wall of partition between us. First, Christ's death tore down the veil which separated God from man. Then He tore down the partition that had separated man from man, race from race.

Notice in verse 15 He abolished in His flesh the enmity between races that had been put forth in the Law (which had commanded separation until the birth of the Seed). Then He took of those two — Jew and Gentile — and made in Himself one new man or race, so making peace.

Peace has been made between the races. God has His Savior in the earth and the "bounds of habitation," the middle wall of partition, has been removed. God in Christ has created a new creature, not known after the flesh but after the Spirit.

Then in verse 16 we see that Christ has reconciled the races to God in one body, and we all have access to God by one Spirit. Jesus was telling this to the Samaritan woman: that the day would come when all men, regardless of race, would worship the Father in spirit and in truth.

After Messiah, no race has a monopoly on access to God or to His covenants and promises. There is "equal access" for all in Christ. No more going to Jerusalem and being treated as second-class citizens. No more sitting in the balcony or outer court. As verse 19 says:

> **Now therefore ye are no more strangers and foreigners, but fellowcitizens with the saints, and of the household of God.**

The Only Way to True Equality

As I stated earlier, the purpose of genealogies is not to trace *racial* heritage but *family* heritage (Ephesians 3:14,15).

As long as we have faith in Christ, we have been adopted into the family of Abraham. We are heirs of God and joint-heirs with Christ (Romans 8:17).

Reconciliation puts everyone on an equal basis, taking no account of the past. The key is understanding that the flesh has to die in order for reconciliation to occur. Carnal, fleshly thinking prohibits the reconciliation process from becoming a reality to Christians.

While we *see* one another after the flesh — Black, White, Hispanic, Indian, Oriental — we must *know* one another after the flesh no more. We must view people in the way that God views them. The Scripture states it this way: **...the Lord seeth not as man seeth; for man looketh on the outward appearance, but the Lord looketh on the heart** (1 Samuel 16:7). We only know the reconciled new creature that has been crucified and raised with Christ.

Reconciliation is the only way to true equality. It brings us to fellowship, seeing one another in the same class or level as ourselves. First John 1:3 speaks of our ability to fellowship with one another as well as with God. This means we are not to feel inferior to other people or to God in terms of class.

Certainly we are inferior to God before the new birth; however, because of Christ, in Him we are **accepted in the beloved** (Ephesians 1:6). We can commune with Him and **be partakers of the divine nature** (2 Peter 1:4).

So all feelings of fear, inferiority and inadequacy are gone because the consciousness of sin is gone. We can stand in God's presence without fear.

Likewise, reconciliation between races eliminates feelings of inferiority. In Christ, the races have fellowship one with another. Reconciliation means being able to stand in the presence of those of another race without any fear, intimidation or feelings of inferiority. It is being able to look one another in the eye and shake hands with feelings of equality and respect.

When one race feels superior to another, reconciliation has not taken effect. Similarly, when one race feels inferior to another, reconciliation still has not taken effect.

The Ministry of Reconciliation

Let's look at some verses from Second Corinthians:

> **For the love of Christ constraineth us; because we thus judge, that if one died for all, then were all dead:**
>
> **And that he died for all, that they which live should not henceforth live unto themselves, but unto him which died for them, and rose again.**
>
> **Wherefore henceforth know we no man after the flesh: yea, though we have known Christ after the flesh, yet now henceforth know we him no more.**
>
> **Therefore if any man be in Christ, he is a new creature: old things are passed away; behold, all things are become new.**
>
> **And all things are of God, who hath reconciled us to himself by Jesus Christ, and hath given to us the ministry of reconciliation.**
>
> **2 Corinthians 5:14-18**

Again, the emphasis is upon the work Christ did to bring about reconciliation. In order for the benefit to manifest, we must consider ourselves to have died with Christ. Since He died for all (representing all), then all died with Him. We, therefore, cannot live for ourselves anymore, because we are dead. Our flesh — no matter what color it may be — is dead in Him.

As Paul says, **...henceforth know we no man after the flesh** (v. 16), and neither do we know Christ after the flesh. He knows us by faith, not by sight. Likewise, we must know our brothers and sisters by faith and not by sight.

If any man is in Christ, he is a new creature — a new species of being that never before existed. Certainly with the carnal mind we can see the skin color. But as we make a decision to know each other by the Spirit rather than by the flesh, the power of reconciliation kicks in.

Then, as Paul says, we have been given the ministry of reconciliation. In the body of Christ, we are first to be reconciled (or to be as one). We cannot help the world solve its ethnic problems if we in the body cannot be reconciled as one.

In John 17:11 Jesus prayed to the Father for us, **...that they may be one, even as we are.** Jesus wants us to be one, as He and the Father are one.

Even as the races were at peace before the Tower of Babel, the word *reconciliation* means we can be at peace again. *Re-* means again and *conciliation* means being at peace.

In Genesis 11:1 the people of that day were of one speech, so they acted as one. Then on the Day of Pentecost, every man heard others speaking in his own language (Acts 2:5-11). Although the apostle Peter's explanation for this event was to fulfill Joel's prophecy, it is this author's opinion that it also serves as a sign of God's reconciling the nations again (Isaiah 28:11; 1 Corinthians 14:21,22).

The curse of the Tower of Babel has been removed. Messiah, Jesus, the Anointed One, has come; and the time of the gathering and reconciling of nations has come. Racial separation is no longer necessary and is unacceptable; peace and goodwill toward all men is in order.

A Call to Unity

We are experiencing in these last days in the body of Christ a call to unity for the sake of the anointing. While nations are rising against nation, we in the body of Christ must come together in order to preach the Gospel to all nations.

We are experiencing the restitution of all things as nations are regaining their old identities and ancient cultures are being revived. As ethnic walls are being rebuilt in the natural, they are coming down in the body of Christ.

We cannot allow again the pull of modern culture to dictate our choices in matters pertaining to race. As the world becomes more segregated and polarized, the body of Christ must become reconciled.

Christ is the Mediator between God and man, and between man and man. He has become the bridge and the door. To get to God, man must come through Him. To get to man, man must come through Him. He is the Mediator, the Go-between, the Umpire between God and man. All other mediators are impostors, powerbrokers drawing men unto themselves.

The hope of the entire world hinges upon the Church communicating the great truth of First Timothy 2:5, which says:

For there is one God, and one mediator between God and men, the man Christ Jesus.

If the nations would look to Christ as Mediator, the common basis for peace would be brought forth.

If the descendants of Shem, Ham and Japheth would realize that Christ is the Common Mediator, then strife in the Middle East would end.

Likewise, in the realm of the races in America, strife and division would cease if all would look to Christ as Mediator.

The Muslims and Serbs in Bosnia would be at peace if they were reconciled to Christ and then to each other in Christ.

Reconciliation is the key to race relations, requiring that we know no man anymore after the flesh. We all are made of one blood, and in Christ we are of one Spirit. We are reconciled or brought together in Christ Jesus. The hostility, fear and enmity is done away with in Him.

With reconciliation comes restitution. When the prodigal son came back to his father, he was reconciled, and restitution was made (Luke 15:21-24).

Let us now look at *restitution,* at what it entails and how it will affect the nations and the Church in the future.

As previously mentioned, nations are being restored to their original state or territories. Most notable, of course, is Israel; but also Germany, the former Soviet republic. The Antichrist is gathering his nations together for one-world government, but likewise Jesus Christ is gathering His nation, the Church. We are not seeing the restitution of all things taking place. Let's take a closer look at this.

6
The Restitution of All Things

Repent ye therefore, and be converted, that your sins may be blotted out, when the times of refreshing shall come from the presence of the Lord;

And he shall send Jesus Christ, which before was preached unto you:

Whom the heaven must receive until the times of restitution of all things, which God hath spoken by the mouth of all his holy prophets since the world began.

Acts 3:19-21

Notice that in this passage it says Christ cannot return **until the times of restitution of all things.** The word *restitution,* in effect, entails restoration plus damages. That means in these last days God is going to restore all things to their original state, causing restitution to be made as well.

The Restitution Process Is Underway

The prophet Haggai said God would shake all nations (Haggai 2:6,7). This shaking is taking place now in Europe, in Africa and all over the world. The result is the breaking of the reign of the superpowers and the emergence again of formerly suppressed ethnic groups.

The colonial reigns of Great Britain, France and other European nations are being slowly lifted. With this will come a rise in ethnicity. This restitution will cause nations to repossess their inheritance and be restored to their lands. God will also cause restitution to be made to these nations. Israel's return to its land was the sign of the beginning of this period.

The significant use of Black ministries and churches in America is a part of that restitution. God is reconciling the books and balancing the accounts. The rapid increase in knowledge and accessibility to it has greatly sped up this restitution process.

More and more, we will see God sovereignly raising up ministries, with individuals and races learning to use their own faith to receive their inheritance from God.

It's Time to Come Together!

In the midst of this restitution, it is not surprising that Satan would conspire to bring about an increasing amount of division and separation.

While God wants to be glorified by seeing people becoming self-sufficient and rejoicing in their own work, emerging ministries must learn not to "bite the hand that fed them."

I have heard some Black ministers say arrogantly, "This is the hour for the Black man to be used by God. The White man's time has passed."

In many parts of the world, Western cultivation and influences are on the decline. However, it is rather shallow to assume that Blacks will become dominant while Whites take on a recessive role. The Church simply does not work in that fashion.

God has a higher purpose in restitution than striving over issues of superiority. This restitution has to do with preparing the body of Christ in America for the overall changing ethnic environment. Jesus' prophecy of nation against nation and kingdom against kingdom is rapidly being fulfilled (Matthew 24:6-8).

It is quite possible that this rise in ethnicity may preclude certain races from having access to others. Changes in places such as Africa and the Caribbean may present political barriers that could jeopardize the mission efforts of White ministries. Such would necessitate the availability of strong Black-led mission efforts. While this may seem far-fetched at this time, dramatic changes in the geopolitical realm are imminent.

Even in America, where racial tension and ethnicity are on the rise, the need for strong Black ministries is more pronounced than ever. With the federal government cutting back on social programs and an atmosphere of global expedience taking precedence over local concerns, only the intervention of the Church will prevent major upheaval among the races.

The whole world is going through a transition. Only if the Church is strong in its ministry to all races will the demands of our changing world be met. It is important that the distribution of resources, the sharing of anointings and mutual respect be of prime interest in today's Church.

We can ill afford prideful contentions between the races at such a crucial time.

This is no time for White brethren to teach "uppity Blacks" a lesson by withdrawing from those who are assertive and poignant in their style and personality.

This is no time for Blacks to try to prove they are not "Uncle Toms" or "house boys" by becoming excessive with ethnically driven verbiage and sermons that emphasize differences rather than unity.

We must not become diverted from the true purpose for restitution, which is empowerment — empowerment to preach the Gospel.

Empowerment To Preach

But thou shalt remember the Lord thy God: for it is he that giveth thee power to get wealth, that he may establish his covenant which he sware unto thy fathers, as it is this day.

Deuteronomy 8:18

The purpose for the restoration of rights and privileges for all races is to enable them to spread the Gospel.

For the first time since Philip shared the Gospel with the Ethiopian eunuch, the Black man is finding himself on the cutting edge of the privilege of spreading the Gospel. (See Acts 8:27-39.)

Each time the Spirit of God has tried to stir Black churches into spreading the Gospel that effort has been turned into a social movement, a "good-time club," a "glorified-preacher society."

This empowerment by God was sent to enable the Church to preach the Gospel to *all* nations.

Remember, God made a covenant with Abram (Abraham), stating that he would be a blessing to all the nations of the earth. For Abraham to be a blessing, he had to be blessed, or endowed. God said to him:

> **And I will make of thee a great nation, and I will bless thee, and make thy name great; and thou shalt be a blessing.**
> **Genesis 12:2**

Why did God do this? Because Abraham, in effect, became a Gospel preacher. This description of Abraham is not out of line with Scripture. In Genesis 12 "Abram" misled Pharaoh concerning his wife; and at that point, he was not a prophet. But in Genesis 20 there is a similar situation with Abimelech in which God says of Abraham, **...for he is a prophet...** (v. 7). This is the first time the word *prophet* is used in Scripture. The Hebrew word here means "inspired man or prophet."[1] It is the same word used for every other Old Testament prophet.

A Divine Principle

No believer is bound to obey; but we are bound by covenant to do so. The Mosaic Law demanded it (Leviticus

---

[1]Strong, "Hebrew and Chaldee Dictionary," p. 75, #5030.

27:30; Malachi 3:10). The apostle Paul brought this out clearly in First Corinthians 9:9-14. In fact, in Second Corinthians 12:13, he apologized to the Corinthians for not being more forward concerning this spiritual law. He said this was the one area in which they were inferior to other churches (2 Corinthians 8:7). Many missionaries make this same mistake today crippling or at least hindering the grace of God from flourishing toward developing nations.

The hearer is under tribute to the preacher. God challenged the Israelites to preach the Gospel and promised them that, if they were faithful, other nations would submit to them. That is why Jesus said, **It is more blessed to give than to receive** (Acts 20:35).

Look at Haiti, for example. There are probably more missionaries per capita in this impoverished nation than perhaps any other. But the people there will stay impoverished until they make the transition from always receiving to giving out. When they begin sending out missionaries to the world, they will be blessed.

The African continent, with the exception of a few areas, is largely the same. It is richer in natural resources than any other land, yet its people are constantly struggling to stay above poverty. Why? Because it receives in more than it gives out.

There is a divine principle brought out in Scripture that is very profound. It is this: The wealth of the world will follow the people who preach the Gospel.

Trace the history of the Gospel, or the Word of God. Because Israel had the Law, its people were blessed above all people. However, when they turned from God, became stiffnecked and served other gods, they fell under a curse.

The Early Church (pre-Pauline the first thirty years) was composed almost exclusively of Jews. In Jerusalem, the believers were heavily persecuted by the unbelieving religious hierarchy as the message of Christ was largely rejected by the Jews. This persecution became so intense that Jewish believers became dependent upon the Gentile churches for their support (Acts 15; Galatians 2:9,10).

Isaiah had prophesied of the time when Gentiles would come to their light and the wealth of the Gentiles would come with them. (Isaiah 60:5.) This double-reference Scripture will be fulfilled in its fullness during the reign of Christ.

Ultimately, due to Israel's overall rejection of the Gospel, the nation was scattered in 70 A.D. and did not gather again officially until 1948. Ironically, it was Satan's persecution of the Church and its subsequent scattering from Jerusalem of those **devout men, out of every nation under heaven** (Acts 2:5) that led to the spread of the Gospel, as these devout men went back to their own lands.

In Acts, chapter 8, we see the account of Philip preaching to the Ethiopian eunuch. As a result, the blessing of Abraham came to the continent of Africa. At this point, the descendants of Shem (the Israelites and Samaritans) and Ham (African people) have been reached with the Gospel. Noah's third son, Japheth, was the progenitor of the White or European people.

Then in Acts, chapter 10, a Roman centurion named Cornelius was presented the Gospel by the apostle Peter. So descendants of Noah's third son, Japheth, were also blessed with the Gospel.

As we look at our world today, it is the European descendents of Japheth who have most aggressively advanced the Gospel. Therefore, it is this author's opinion that there is no coincidence that Western civilization dominates the culture, language and economy of the world. How clearly this demonstrates that Deuteronomy 8:18 is true. God empowers us to get wealth in order to establish His Covenant.

Now it is time to seize and even contend for the right and privilege of preaching the Gospel. God has sent the refreshing of the Spirit to empower all ethnic groups to preach the Gospel.

Unfortunately, in many countries the Gospel has been preached to the people, but the legacy has not been passed on. Nationals must be taught, ordained and sent forth to minister the Gospel to their people and, ultimately, to take it to others. When this cycle is completed, the wealth of the earth will migrate toward those who preach.

Reconciliation is not complete until there is restitution. Restitution is not complete until empowerment is granted to preach the Gospel. As with the prodigal son, restitution was completed when the ring of family authority had been placed upon his finger. He could then do business on behalf of the family with full privilege and authority (Luke 15:22).

Privilege *and* Responsibility

Not only is preaching the Gospel a privilege which begets tribute and honor, it is also a responsibility. It is time for all in the body of Christ to bear their load. The apostle Paul declared this to the Galatian church:

> **But let every man prove his own work, and then shall he have rejoicing in himself alone, and not in another.**
>
> **For every man shall bear his own burden.**
>
> **Galatians 6:4,5**

With the mission fields in Russia and other European countries opening up wide, there obviously has been a shift in priority and resources to get the Gospel into these new hotbeds. Blacks must be in position, as never before, to meet the challenge of preaching the Gospel to developing nations. In doing so, God will provide the resources to get more wealth so that the Gospel will be preached.

Cooperation between races in the body of Christ is essential to making the transition as smooth as possible. As Paul said, it is not right that some men be eased when others are burdened, but that their should be an equality. (2 Corinthians 8:13,14). Restitution is to put all races into a position of blessing and responsibility.

As the vast fields of China and the rest of the Orient open up, God has positioned brethren of other races to harvest their fields. The Caucasian is no longer the only one on the mission field. Every ethnic group is being raised up to meet the challenge of the twenty-first century.

The rise to prominence of the Black man is not a thing of pride but rather a call to accountability. We all must give an account unto God.

Even as free markets of trade are being opened all over the world, so also are great and effectual doors being opened to the Gospel. Those who fail to step out into this new world of opportunity will be isolated and left behind.

In order for us to walk in reconciliation, we must do the ministry of reconciliation. This ministry has been committed to us.

A Dispensation of the Gospel

The apostle Paul commanded Timothy to take that which he had learned and commit it to **faithful men, who shall be able to teach others also** (2 Timothy 2:2).

That is what restitution does: It empowers us to share in the Great Commission and brings equality to all members of the body of Christ.

Notice Paul speaks of committing the Gospel. This denotes that God has allotted or committed the preaching of the Gospel to certain groups of specific people. God ordained certain people to reach certain others. This is called a dispensation of the Gospel.

Observe Paul's words to the Galatian church:

> But contrariwise, when they saw that the gospel of the uncircumcision was *committed* unto me, as the gospel of the circumcision was unto Peter;
>
> (For he that wrought effectually in Peter to the apostleship of the circumcision, the same was mighty in me toward the Gentiles:)
>
> And when James, Cephas, and John, who seemed to be pillars, perceived the grace that was given unto me, they gave to me and Barnabas the right hands of fellowship; that we should go unto the heathen, and they unto the circumcision.
>
> **Galatians 2:7-9**

It is natural and proper that we should reach the people God has given us grace to reach. In fact, He has committed or allocated this portion of the ministry to us. Since it is the grace of God and a direct commission or commitment, then we *have nothing to glory of*. Paul wrote that to the Corinthians:

> For though I preach the gospel, *I have nothing to glory of*: for necessity is laid upon me; yea, woe is unto me, if I preach not the gospel!
>
> For if I do this thing willingly, I have a reward: but if against my will, a dispensation of the gospel is committed unto me.
>
> **1 Corinthians 9:16,17**

Paul would have preferred to be sent to his beloved countrymen, the Jews; but he was drafted to preach to the Gentiles. Peter was called to the Jews.

Paul said to the Corinthians, **Woe is unto me, if I preach not the gospel!** In other words, "A curse will come upon me if I don't preach the Gospel!"

When God promotes us or decides to use us, we, like Paul, have nothing to glory of. God demands a return on

His investment. Instead of ministers being "puffed up," we should be trembling at the awesome responsibility which God has committed to us. We have *nothing* to glory of in ourselves!

The Spirit of Reconciliation

The Black man has greater responsibility now. To whom much is given, much will be required (Luke 12:48). Woe be unto us if we waste this opportunity by arguing over doctrines or spending all of our time on ethnically related issues. There are communities to transform and nations to reach. When God commits a dispensation to us, we are the ones who have to fulfill it.

So it is not unusual that Black ministers generally serve predominantly Black congregations while White ministers serve predominantly White congregations. Some are graced to reach beyond their own race and some are sent to other races.

Nevertheless, the restitution of all things is necessary to ensure that each and every grace required to reach every group is available and functioning.

A dispensation of the Gospel has been committed to ministers within every ethnic group. We must not become diverted from God's ultimate purpose through ignorance. That is why the equality brought about by reconciliation and restitution is so important.

In the midst of this transition, let us remember:

- Don't bite the hand that fed you.

- But neither do you have to kiss it.

- We must look one another in the eye respectfully and shake hands.

That's the spirit of reconciliation.

Equality Through Redistribution

Another aspect of restitution is redistribution of resources. Again, let's look in Galatians, chapter 6:

> Bear ye one another's burdens, and so fulfil the law of Christ.
>
> For if a man think himself to be something, when he is nothing, he deceiveth himself.
>
> But let every man prove his own work, and then shall he have rejoicing in himself alone, and not in another.
>
> For every man shall bear his own burden.
>
> **Galatians 6:2-5**

The misapplication of and disregard for the principles stated in this portion of Scripture is one of the major hindrances to the flow of the corporate anointing. The full grace of God which flows by activation of the anointing is hindered when covetousness or attempt to control enters in.

We must learn to give, making ourselves and our resources available to others — without strings attached.

Methodologies of manipulation and control are oftentimes used by those who have this, hindering the development of wealth and self-sufficiency by those receiving the help. In other cases, the wealth is held back and hoarded by a few who oppress others with grievous burdens. But just as dangerous are those who become like Santa Claus, handing out gifts to every outstretched hand without true regard for long-range growth and development. All of these are wrong uses of wealth and resources.

God is in control of all the wealth of the earth. We, His ministers, are simply stewards over it. As God begins to raise up Blacks and nationals to receive their inheritance by becoming preachers of the Gospel, they must be taught and given the freedom to become fishers of men — not just consumers of the fish and loaves, but fishers and farmers of the Gospel.

To distribute wealth where it is needed, God will speak to men and women, telling them where to give, where to help, even where to worship and submit themselves. This is how the anointing works! God directs and distributes resources according to His desire. We don't own anything; we are just stewards.

During this time of transition in the body of Christ, the Lord is putting together the Church in such a way that distribution will be made to everyone according to need. This is not like communism. It is a covenant. We are fulfilling the law of Christ moving in the anointing.

Although there has been much teaching in this area, few Christians realize the relationship between authority, personal faith, money and the anointing. The anointing cannot flow where there is disorder and broken authority. It cannot flow where the faith of individuals is being dominated. Neither can it flow where money and wealth are not being distributed properly.

His Grace Brings Us Together

Notice these words in Acts, chapter 4:

...and great grace was upon them all.

Neither was there any among them that lacked: for as many as were possessors of lands or houses sold them, and brought the prices of the things that were sold,

And laid them down at the apostles' feet: and distribution was made unto every man according as he had need.

Acts 4:33-35

Verse 33 says that great grace — the fullness of grace — was upon them all. Why? Because the law of Christ (the

Anointing) was being fulfilled. Those who were in need had their needs met, and the Church had revival.

Keep in mind that during this time, according to Acts 2:9-11, there was a multitude of ethnic groups involved. But distribution was made according to the grace given to every person and group.

The New Covenant, governed by the law of Christ, demands that we not think more highly of ourselves than we ought, but that we submit ourselves and the grace in us to the corporate anointing. We are only important because God has given each of us something that someone else needs.

For example, God wants to reach the inner-city groups. One ministry may have the location, while another has the resources. It is neither the ministry with the location nor the ministry with the resources that is preeminent, but God Who gives the increase! (1 Corinthians 3:7). It is only by His anointing that the gangs will be reached. But the anointing will not flow if the ministries do not operate in the law of Christ (the Anointing).

The local pastor has the calling and the location, while the suburban church has the resources which God has allocated to reach that area. But it won't just happen because the inner-city pastor begs for it and the suburban church members are made to feel guilty. The people have to involve themselves through prayer and walking in the Spirit. Then through the corporate anointing, *every* need will be met.

In Acts, chapter 16, we see how the church in Macedonia had prayed and the apostle Paul was instructed by God in a vision to go to them. In that vision Paul saw and heard a man say to him, **Come over into Macedonia, and help us** (v. 9).

Because Paul obeyed, the church in Macedonia became the only church to consistently support his ministry in his final days. (See Philippians 4:15; Acts 16:12.)

Why? Because he went to them under the anointing. Under that anointing, he taught them how to give and to receive — not how to be dependent upon others but how to believe God. Then he allowed them to participate in the spread of the Gospel. As stated earlier, God sends wealth to His people to provide for the preaching of the Gospel.

Becoming Self-Sufficient in Christ

As Paul said in Galatians 6:2, we are to bear one another's burdens (a load too heavy for one to carry alone) and fulfill the law of Christ (the law of the anointing). But then in verse 5 he said:

For every man shall bear his own burden.

You cannot just keep giving fish to people. You must empower them to catch their own fish and become self-sufficient in Christ, the Anointed One.

The word *burden* in this verse is a load that is light enough for one man to carry. Sometimes a need to be in control will cause people to keep others dependent upon them. This hinders the flow of the anointing and grieves the Spirit of God. This is not the law of Christ which leads to freedom. Jesus said, **If the Son therefore shall make you free** (by the anointing)**, ye shall be free indeed** (John 8:36). The anointing liberates the flesh from bondage.

As Galatians 6:4 says:

But let every man prove his own work, and then shall he have rejoicing in himself alone, and not in another.

Self-esteem and self-respect do not come because of skin color, but by success through the anointing of God. As Paul declared, **I can do all things through Christ** (the Anointing) **which strengtheneth me** (Philippians 4:13). It is the Anointing that empowers or strengthens.

The Anointing stepped in when the burden was too heavy to carry. The Anointing taught the principle of sufficiency in Christ. The Anointing proclaimed liberty and the year of release (Luke 4:18,19). Glory to God!

It's time for the body of Christ to flow in the corporate anointing to fulfill the law of Christ. Like the Early Church, great grace will be upon us all; and with great power, we will give witness of the resurrection of our Lord.

Jesus rose, not with a Jewish body (or a black, white, red or yellow body), but with a glorified body. We will give witness of His glorified body when we flow in the corporate anointing and fulfill that law of Christ.

Unfortunately, many do not comprehend this principle, or else they choose to walk contrary to it. Acting alone, they begin to think they are really something when actually they are nothing. A foot is nothing unless it is connected to a body. A hand is nothing unless it is connected to an arm. Likewise, unless we submit to and flow in that which we are anointed to do, we will be useless to the body of Christ. We could actually short-circuit the anointing.

So what am I saying?

A Merging Through Mutual Respect

We are in a time of transition, which is a dangerous time. People can get lost in the shuffle or they can make wrong turns. Things can be misinterpreted or even fall through the cracks. But the major concern is that people may get diverted from the true purpose of God.

During this time, God is going to cause the merging of ministries in both proximity and effort. He will be shifting resources from one place to another. He will speak to Whites to go to predominantly Black churches and Blacks to go to predominantly White churches. In some cases, as I have mentioned, He will cause entire ministries to merge.

Whites will learn to submit to Black leadership and Blacks will learn to respect their own leaders more because of the anointing.

The end result will be a mutual respect and greater appreciation for the calling upon everyone's ministry in the body of Christ.

Those who choose not to flow in the law of Christ will find themselves cut off from the grace of God, because they are not living by the Covenant.

God is demanding equality in the body of Christ. Not everyone having the same thing. Not taking from the rich and giving to the poor. Not pulling down the Whites and giving preeminence to the Blacks. But rather ensuring that every person receives according to the grace and calling on his or her life.

Where much is given, much is required (Luke 12:48). Where much is required, much will be given. We must pray for a revelation of the law of Christ. Then God's anointing will flow in greater power than ever before.

7

Hypocrisy — Seed of Racism

When Peter was come to Antioch, I (Paul) withstood him to the face, because he was to be blamed.

For before that certain came from James, he (Peter) did eat with the Gentiles: but when they were come, he withdrew and separated himself, fearing them which were of the circumcision.

And the other Jews dissembled likewise with him; insomuch that Barnabas also was carried away with their dissimulation.

But when I saw that they walked not uprightly according to the truth of the gospel, I said unto Peter before them all, If thou, being a Jew, livest after the manner of Gentiles, and not as do the Jews, why compellest thou the Gentiles to live as do the Jews?
Galatians 2:11-14

Most of the book thus far has dealt with the issue of Satan conspiring to divide the Church through an overemphasis on ethnicity. As was mentioned, the increased emphasis on ethnicity and culture has caused some to become extreme in their pursuit of matters of natural heritage. If not checked by Scripture, this can be used by Satan to divert people from the faith, even shipwrecking their faith.

In addressing this entire issue, however, we would be less than candid if we did not deal with these ancient nemeses: prejudice and hypocrisy.

In one sense, among minorities there are latent feelings of rejection, opening the door to doctrines that will bolster self-esteem and ethnic pride. Likewise, there are feelings of insecurity by the dominant or majority group, leading to the perpetuation of justifying doctrines of superiority.

While this may be understandable, it is not permissible for the child of God. In fact, knowing what we know about reconciliation and redemption, to continue in these heathenistic patterns is nothing but blatant hypocrisy. We are playacting and pretending to be something we are not in order to satisfy and placate our own race. Such was the case with one of the leading apostles of the Church, Peter.

Peter's Vision

As previously pointed out in this study, Peter was committed to preaching the Gospel to the Jews, while Paul reached out to the Gentiles. Yet in Acts 10 it was Peter who had a visitation from God through a vision. In this vision he saw all kinds of foods which were not lawful for Jews to eat. Let's look at this incident in the Scriptures:

> On the morrow, as they went on their journey, and drew nigh unto the city, Peter went up upon the housetop to pray about the sixth hour:
>
> And he became very hungry, and would have eaten: but while they made ready, he fell into a trance,
>
> And saw heaven opened, and a certain vessel descending unto him, as it had been a great sheet knit at the four corners, and let down to the earth:
>
> Wherein were all manner of fourfooted beasts of the earth, and wild beasts, and creeping things, and fowls of the air.
>
> And there came a voice to him, Rise, Peter; kill, and eat.
>
> But Peter said, Not so, Lord; for I have never eaten any thing that is common or unclean.
>
> And the voice spake unto him again the second time, What God hath cleansed, that call not thou common.

> **This was done thrice: and the vessel was received up again into heaven.**
>
> **Acts 10:9-16**

In this vision God was saying to Peter, "Do not call as unclean what I have called clean."

Now we must understand that for years God had separated the Jewish people from the remainder of the world. He gave them strict dietary laws and forbade them from intermingling with people who did not serve their God. He did this, not because they were better than other people, but because the Messiah was to come through their lineage. He preserved them because of His promise to Abraham.

But viewing themselves as God's special people seriously affected their attitude. Being easily diverted, they adopted a demeanor of superiority. They considered other nations to be as dogs. They saw those people as unclean barbarians. In other words, there was deep-rooted bigotry and prejudice abiding in them.

Peter's Attitude

When Peter had this vision, God showed it to him three different times to confirm its meaning. But due to deep-rooted prejudice, Peter still doubted. So God sent to him the men he had seen in the vision. They escorted him to Cornelius's house where the people were meeting together. The Scripture says of Peter:

> **And he said unto them, Ye know how that it is an unlawful thing for a man that is a Jew to keep company, or come unto one of another nation; but God hath shewed me that I should not call any man common or unclean.**
>
> **Acts 10:28**

Notice how Peter immediately let Cornelius know the way things usually were. In this verse he was saying: "I'm really not supposed to keep company with you people. But God told me not to call you by your name, so I won't."

How prevalent this protective attitude is today. We know the Word of God forbids us from looking down on other people, but we simply annotate what God said and then keep living the way our society teaches us. This is tokenism and hypocrisy.

Jesus said of hypocrites:

> **This people draweth nigh unto me with their mouth, and honoureth me with their lips; but their heart is far from me.**
>
> **Matthew 15:8**

Peter was explaining how honored Cornelius should be because he came under his roof. When Peter had first entered the room, Cornelius, just as affected by this societal-class grooming, fell down and worshipped him (Acts 10:25).

How powerful are the images of racism and prejudice. We find ourselves acting it out without thinking. The damage that these images do to the minds of people is greater than what most people can imagine. That image was so strong in Peter that God had to show him another image three times in that vision. How important it is that people see the right picture of God's plan for race relations. A picture is more valuable than 20,000 empty words.

Then while there in Cornelius's house, Peter opened his mouth and declared:

> **...Of a truth I perceive that God is no respecter of persons:**
>
> **But in every nation he that feareth him, and worketh righteousness, is accepted with him.**
>
> **Acts 10:34,35**

As Peter continued to preach, the Holy Ghost fell upon Cornelius and his house. Peter knew then, beyond any doubt, that God had accepted them.

His Brethren's Reaction

In Acts 11, Peter went back to headquarters and reported to the holy brethren what has happened. Peter again seemed defensive, saying:

> **Forasmuch then as God gave them the like gift as he did unto us, who believed on the Lord Jesus Christ; what was I, that I could withstand God?**
>
> **Acts 11:17**

The next verse simply says:

> **When they heard these things, they held their peace, and glorified God, saying, Then hath God also to the Gentiles granted repentance unto life** (v. 18).

They honored God, but as verse 18 says, **They held their peace.** They really had no comment.

There is no mention of anyone saying, "Praise God! The walls have fallen! Now we can fellowship with the Gentiles!"

Their response was more like, "I guess God can do whatever He wants to. He's God, and there's nothing we can do to stop it."

In summary, their hearts were not in it.

Peter's Example of Hypocrisy

Having this background, we can now deal with this passage and understand Paul's displeasure with Peter.

In Galatians, chapter 2, Paul writes about his confrontation with Peter in Antioch (v. 11). It seems Peter had been eating with the Gentiles. I can just see him: finishing up a big plate of chitterlings and turnip greens cooked with bacon drippings. He was having a great time!

Then, in walk some of his brethren from Jerusalem. Immediately, Peter jumps up from the table, wipes that pork chop grease from his face and pretends that he was not eating with the Gentiles. Barnabas, taking his cue from Peter, also pretends, acting the same way (vv. 12,13).

With Barnabas, this shows how people tend to follow their leader. Leaders will answer to God for the example they put before others.

Children Are Taught Hypocrisy

Parents who have taught their children to be prejudiced toward other ethnic groups will also be answering to God for their hypocrisy.

For example, one White child may observe his merchant father freely accepting money for merchandise from people of another race in a store located in that community. But later he hears his father say, "You had better watch those people closely — they will steal from you!" What kind of message does that send?

The very damaging and hypocritical lesson he learned from his father was that all Blacks are slick criminals, shiftless and lazy; you can accept their money, but you can't accept their person.

A Black child may hear his parent say, "All White folks are devils!" What impression does that leave the child as he waves goodbye to his father going to work for "the devil"? With that background, he grows up feeling the system is corrupt and loaded against him. As a result, he drops out of school, rebels against the law, ends up in the White man's jail and becomes a Black Muslim.

More important than these two examples are thoughts such as: What kind of impression is the Church leaving? Is the fact that the local Church remains one of the least-integrated institutions in America any indication of hypocrisy?

Being a Respecter of Persons

As Peter said, **Of a truth I perceive that God is no respecter of persons** (Acts 10:34). He spoke those words with his mouth, but his heart wasn't in it. God is *not* a respecter of persons, but Peter and his Jewish friends were. They were too steeped in prejudice to accept that they had misunderstood God's will all along.

The Law never told the Jewish people to be respecters of persons, but tradition did. In fact, the apostle James said:

> **My brethren, have not the faith of our Lord Jesus Christ, the Lord of glory, with respect of persons.**
> **James 2:1**

We should never have the faith of our Lord Jesus Christ with respect of persons. As James points out, the goal of the Law was to love our neighbor as ourselves:

> **If ye fulfil the royal law according to the scripture, Thou shalt love thy neighbour as thyself, ye do well.**
> **James 2:8**

As verse 9 says:

> **But if ye have respect to persons, ye commit sin, and are convinced of the law as transgressors.**

This means we are guilty of breaking the whole Law. What a powerful indictment!

The Church's Responsibility for Racial Acceptance

Likewise, it is tradition and cultural pressure that has caused the Church to lag behind society in this area. We are afraid our children will intermarry, or the rich will be offended, or our property will be destroyed, or our purses will be stolen. And God forbid that we should have to put *them* into leadership or put up with *those* worship styles!

While we preach scathing sermons about the liberal religious tradition of other churches, we draw nigh with our mouths but our hearts are far from how God really feels.

As Paul rebuked Peter, saying he was to blame for the dissimulation of the others, likewise it is today's ministers who are to blame for the Church's feeble efforts toward racial acceptance and fellowship. This includes Blacks as much as Whites.

Relationship Brings Criticism

In my home city of North Little Rock, Arkansas, I maintain fellowship with a most respected and trusted friend, Pastor Happy Caldwell of Agape Church. I frequently co-host his television program or fill in for him. Our relationship is strong enough that he trusts me to do his program when he is away. We always endeavor to portray in a non-carnal, non-choreographed way the trusting, honest, wholesome relationship that should exist between Blacks and Whites, especially the leaders.

To my surprise, I came under great criticism and attack from other Black ministers. I was called names like *Happy's boy, Uncle Tom, Cheese-eater, house boy* and a host of other such terms. Happy also came under fire for his relationship with me, for allowing me to be honest and candid, and for relating to me on an equal basis.

People who are carnally minded never seem to see the spiritual applications. Many Black ministers wanted me to use this opportunity as a forum to harp on racial issues and differences rather than focus on the Gospel. Far too often, this has been the case as we continue to dwell on the past, opening old wounds and harping on the same old injustices and misdeeds.

We have chosen rather to set an example of how ministries can work together by the inspiration of the Holy Spirit, not for some shallow, contrived, political "dog and pony" show.

Suffice it to say that there is as much reluctance toward integration of churches on the Black side as there is on the White side, but for totally different reasons.

I have shared this about Happy and myself so that others will know they cannot allow pressure to stop them from obeying God. It hurts to be misunderstood and wrongly accused when you are doing what is right.

Regarding the apostle Peter and his instruction from God to accept uncircumcised Gentiles, he knew what was right. But pressure from his peers, traditional thinking and his own reluctance to walk in the revelation God had given him caused him to be hypocritical. He experienced the joy of fellowshipping with the Gentiles, but then he was faced with the uncomfortable position of having to explain those relationships to his comrades. So he chose to deny them. What hypocrisy! He allowed the pressures of prejudice and racism to cause him to be ashamed of his new-found brothers and sisters in the Lord.

Nicodemus Protected His Reputation, Too

This reminds me of Nicodemus. The Scripture says:

> **There was a man of the Pharisees, named Nicodemus, a ruler of the Jews:**
>
> **The same came to Jesus by night, and said unto him, Rabbi, we know that thou art a teacher come from God: for no man can do these miracles that thou doest, except God be with him.**
>
> **John 3:1,2**

The Pharisees and scribes had decided to have nothing to do with Jesus, but Nicodemus knew there was something very real about Him. Having seen the miracles He performed and hearing the revelation by which He spoke, Nicodemus called Him *Rabbi*, or Master, a teacher from God. But knowing all of this, he still wanted to protect his reputation, so it was at night that he came to talk with Jesus.

We Must Be Genuine With Others

How many today are secretly fellowshipping under the cover of the dark, not wanting to be identified as fellowshipping with "those people"? Even worse, how many pretend to fellowship publicly, but privately still harbor feelings of prejudice and bigotry?

God's Word tells us that we are to love without dissimulation (Romans 12:9). Pretense and hypocrisy stink in the nostrils of God. We must be sincere in our relationships and honest in our communication with one another.

Whatever I do in public must be genuine and not tokenistic. Likewise, my reputation should be able to bear publicly anything I am willing to do privately.

The apostle Peter and much of the Early Church failed the test of respect of persons. It is not easy to "unteach" people the things they have been taught over many years. Tradition is so strong that it can make even the Word of God of none effect (Mark 7:13).

Continued prejudice over a protracted period of time may produce an attitude of malice and ill will. To be constantly maligned and treated differently (which is discrimination) just because one is of a certain skin color can produce anger. This anger can lead to racial violence and hatred. Let's look at an example of this in Scripture.

"Ye Know Not What Manner of Spirit Ye Are Of"

And it came to pass, when the time was come that he (Jesus) should be received up, he stedfastly set his face to go to Jerusalem,

And sent messengers before his face: and they went, and entered into a village of the Samaritans, to make ready for him.

> And they did not receive him, because his face was as though he would go to Jerusalem.
>
> And when his disciples James and John saw this, they said, Lord, wilt thou that we command fire to come down from heaven, and consume them, even as Elias did?
>
> But he turned, and rebuked them, and said, Ye know not what manner of spirit ye are of.
>
> For the Son of man is not come to destroy men's lives, but to save them. And they went to another village.
>
> And it came to pass, that, as they went in the way, a certain man said unto him, Lord, I will follow thee whithersoever thou goest.
>
> And Jesus said unto him, Foxes have holes, and birds of the air have nests; but the Son of man hath not where to lay his head.
>
> Luke 9:51-58

Even Jesus was a victim of racism, being denied a place to stay by Samaritans because He was a Jew. The New Testament in basic English says Jesus was clearly going to Jerusalem. The fact that He was going to Jerusalem to worship identified Him as a Jew. Because the Samaritans were "mixed" Jews, there was no clear way to make distinction by skin coloration. The term *face* in verse 53 simply means "outward appearance."[1] So Jesus and His party gave some indication that they were going to Jerusalem to worship.

As John 4:9,20-23 indicates, the Jews and Samaritans had long been at odds about where and how God should be worshiped and they had no dealings with each other. Because the Samaritans had intermarried with their races, the Jews considered them as dogs. The ethnic and cultural

---

[1]Strong, "Greek Dictionary of the New Testament," p. 62, #4383.

distinctions were very pronounced, leading to this confrontation.[2]

How ironic that the Creator of the universe found Himself rejected because of racial bigotry.

Jesus' followers were so offended that they wanted to start a race war. James and John, who were called **the sons of thunder** (Mark 3:17), said, "Lord, let's call fire out of heaven and burn this place down!"

To this, Jesus replied, **Ye know not what manner of spirit ye are of** (v. 55).

It was that same mind-set — a mind-set of vengeance — that set the blazes in Watts, both in the '60s and the '90s.

There is a mind-set that wants to retaliate against the injustice of prejudice and bigotry: a mind-set of malice and hatred.

I see many Christian leaders in the Afro-American community today who have allowed this spirit to overtake them. They, like James and John, are calling down the fire of vengeance upon their "foes."

There are many people who don't know what it is to be discriminated against, being denied privileges and rights solely because of one's ethnic background. It is dehumanizing, demoralizing and degrading.

But we can take consolation or warning in the fact that our Lord knows what it is like.

How it must grieve Him that even the animal and fowl kingdoms — the foxes and birds — can dwell together, but the Son of Man Himself found no place to dwell because of bigotry. Foxes can have holes while birds have nests in the same tree, but man has yet to understand that we all are of one blood.

---

[2]Curtis, p. 2019.

The woman at the well, whom we mentioned earlier, was hesitant to give Jesus a drink because of racial tension between these same groups, the Jews and the Samaritans. It was the Jews normally having the superior attitude who prompted the woman to say, **How is it that thou, being a Jew, askest drink of me, which am a woman of Samaria? for the Jews have no dealings with the Samaritans** (John 4:9). Later in that chapter, it says when the disciples returned and heard His conversation with her, they **marvelled that he talked with the woman** (v. 27), but they said nothing.

Ironically, it was these same apostles who were reluctant to obey Christ's commandment to go to Samaria and to the uttermost parts of the world. It was only when persecution hit that a deacon named Philip went into Samaria to preach.

Could they not remember the example that Christ set with this woman at the well? Could it be that the same attitude which had come on the "sons of thunder" continued to hinder them?

This attitude of ill will and malice still plagues people 2,000 years later. How do we deal with this?

"Let the Dead Bury the Dead"

Malice, bitterness and hatred are the catalysts that fuel ethnic strife. These horrible poisons are the result of unforgiveness. Unforgiveness is the state of keeping past offenses active rather than putting them in the "dead file."

In the passage from Luke's gospel, chapter 9, Jesus emphasizes how important it is to properly dispose of ethnic offenses if we are to follow Him. Let's continue with verse 59:

> **And he (Jesus) said unto another, Follow me. But he said, Lord, suffer me first to go and bury my father.**
>
> **Jesus said unto him, Let the dead bury their dead: but go thou and preach the kingdom of God.**

> And another also said, Lord, I will follow thee; but
> let me first go bid them farewell, which are at home at
> my house.
>
> And Jesus said unto him, No man, having put his
> hand to the plough, and looking back, is fit for the
> kingdom of God.
>
> **Luke 9:59-62**

Jesus makes it clear that in order to follow Him we cannot be preoccupied with "dead issues." An unforgiving spirit never lets offenses die.

Some people are still flying the Confederate flag and singing *Dixie*, while others continually rehearse the horrors of slavery and discrimination. They just won't let it die. Some claim that they have let it die, but they are still "wearing their funeral clothes and preaching the eulogy."

Jesus was saying, "Let the dead bury the dead — we are going to preach the kingdom." How can we who have put our hand to the plow of reconciliation be effective if we keep looking back?

Some will be angry at these words and say, "No, brother, we must never forget!"

But we are not talking about forgetting history; we are talking about forgiving the people. We may not forget the act, but we must forgive the person who committed the act. What a drastic difference there is between the two! Forgiveness is the entrance to reconciliation.

Attitudes and Feelings to Avoid

Notice Paul's words in Ephesians, chapter 4:

> Let all bitterness, and wrath (which is retaliation),
> and anger, and clamour, and evil speaking, be put away
> from you, with all malice:
>
> And be ye kind one to another, tenderhearted,
> forgiving one another, even as God for Christ's sake
> (the Anointing's sake) hath forgiven you.
>
> **Ephesians 4:31,32**

Bitterness, wrath, anger, clamour, evil speaking and malice — all are a result of unforgiveness. Let's consider each of these.

Bitterness

Bitterness is dangerous because it is like a virus. Medical doctors say that viruses are the most infectious and rapidly spreading diseases.

When ministers become bitter, they can set off a plague because they affect so many people. Little wonder that, as Hebrews 12:15 says, many are defiled by bitterness. Look at verses 14 and 15:

Follow peace with all men, and holiness, without which no man shall see the Lord:

Looking diligently lest any man fail of the grace of God; lest any root of bitterness springing up trouble you, and thereby many be defiled.

The Word says we must diligently pursue peace, or reconciliation, to prevent bitterness.

Wrath

We are reminded in Romans 12:19 AMP to **...never avenge yourselves, but leave the way open for [God's] wrath; for it is written, Vengeance is Mine, I will repay (requite), says the Lord.**

James 1:20 says, **For the wrath of man worketh not the righteousness of God.**

When we begin to take vengeance into our own hands, this does not work the righteousness of God. Dr. Martin Luther King, Jr. proved that it is better to walk in peace and not avenge oneself. Oh, that we would learn to walk in the Spirit and know that **when a man's ways please the Lord, he maketh even his enemies to be at peace with him** (Proverbs 16:7). Wrath is reserved for God Himself.

Anger and Clamor

Paul admonishes us to put away anger. Ephesians 4:26 says:

> **Be ye angry, and sin not: let not the sun go down upon your wrath.**

Here Paul is making reference to Psalm 4:4, which says:

> **Stand in awe, and sin not: commune with your own heart upon your bed, and be still.**

The Lord is saying that it is natural to be angry at sin and injustice. Righteous indignation causes us to stand in awe (shock and amazement), to abhor sin and to marvel at how blatantly people disregard the Word of God and mistreat others.

But we are warned not to speak or act out of anger. It says, **Stand in awe, and sin not....** Speaking or acting in anger will only precipitate clamor.

Clamor is the same as uproar, disturbance, strife and confusion. How quickly something can get out of hand and turn into a full-scale war if anger is not handled properly.

The word *awe* also means we must reverence and fear God in such a way that our conduct brings honor to Him. No matter how angry we become by the wrongdoings of others, we must sanctify God before men.

The greatest example of one's failure to do this is Moses. Moses became angry with the children of Israel, and he smote the rock rather than speaking to it as God commanded. He spoke in haste and anger, conducting himself in a manner not befitting a leader. God relieved Moses of his command because he (Moses) failed to "sanctify" Him before the people (Numbers 20:12).

We must order our steps by the Word of God, not by our feelings and emotions. Outbursts of anger and irresponsible language will not only stir up anger in an opponent but bring a reproach upon Christ, especially when the leaders are highly visible.

The body of Christ will have ample opportunity to get into racial strife as we approach the end times. Satan has the political and social worlds at odds with each other to the degree that violence could break out at any moment. These forces will apply great pressure upon the body of Christ to choose sides and divide into camps. Satan wants to open up old wounds and stir up anger to the point of provocation.

If we really fear God and reverence the anointing, we will sanctify Him and not take liberties for ourselves. Moses and Aaron lost the anointing of God because they failed to reverence Him and His anointing.

Psalm 4:4 then says: **...commune with your own heart upon your bed....** Instead of acting, we must commune with our own heart. We must not confer and speak with others in anger. When one is angry and upset, it tends to attract other people who are angry and upset. Rather than disarming the anger, they support and encourage one another in it. It is far better to commune with one's own heart, meditate on the Word and get back into the Spirit.

The apostle Peter put it this way:

> **But sanctify the Lord God in your hearts: and be ready always to give an answer to every man that asketh you a reason of the hope that is in you with meekness and fear.**
>
> **1 Peter 3:15**

David's final admonition in Psalm 4:4 is: **...and be still.**

Notice Psalm 37:7-11:

> **Rest in the Lord, and wait patiently for him: fret not thyself because of him who prospereth in his way, because of the man who bringeth wicked devices to pass.**

> **Cease from anger, and forsake wrath: fret not thyself in any wise to do evil.**
>
> **For evildoers shall be cut off: but those that wait upon the Lord, they shall inherit the earth.**
>
> **For yet a little while, and the wicked shall not be: yea, thou shalt diligently consider his place, and it shall not be.**
>
> **But the meek shall inherit the earth; and shall delight themselves in the abundance of peace.**

To be still is to rest in the Lord and let Him be God. We are to cease from anger, forsake wrath and in no wise think to do evil.

Verse 9 says, **For evildoers shall be cut off....** For Christians, this means the anointing will be cut off. Even though the gifts and calling of God are without repentance (Romans 11:29), if a believer continually engages in any sin, including regularly operating in anger and wrath, he may lose his anointing until he deals with the sin. I tremble to think that some may lose their anointing because they are operating in anger and wrath.

While the rest of the world is caught up in ethnic strife, we must "be still," honor God, honor Christ Jesus and honor the Anointing.

I can even see the anointing now waning on some of the visible leaders in the body of Christ. Their attitudes and dispositions before the people are not pleasing to God. Their messages are becoming more and more divisive; and the undertones of bitterness, wrath and anger are obvious.

Although injustice and evil doing may have provoked the anger, it is not being put away or disposed of according to the Word. This is causing clamor, gatherings, evil speaking, surmising and potentially irreparable division in the body. Likewise, those who continue to practice racism and bigotry will not be used of God in the last days. God will not tolerate these attitudes.

Evil Speaking

Speak not evil one of another, brethren. He that speaketh evil of his brother, and judgeth his brother, speaketh evil of the law, and judgeth the law: but if thou judge the law, thou art not a doer of the law, but a judge.

James 4:11

We are commanded in the Word of God that we are not to speak evil concerning another brother. The *New Berkeley Version* says, **Do not malign one another.**[3] We are not to speak critically or judgmentally of another. To do so is to speak a curse upon our brother. It is like "throwing stones" of condemnation. When we condemn others, we bring condemnation on ourselves. Why? Because James says when we criticize others we become a judge of the Law and not a doer of it. We have exalted ourselves to judge, jury and executioner.

Notice the preceding verse, James 4:10, says: **Humble yourselves in the sight of the Lord, and he shall lift you up.** Speaking evil is a sign of pride and conceit.

Remember when the scribes and Pharisees caught the woman in adultery? (John 8:3-11). They were ready to throw stones, but Jesus took His finger and began to write in the dirt. That finger was the same finger that wrote the Ten Commandments in stone on Mount Sinai. He was saying, "I am the only Lawgiver and Judge." Then He said to them, **He that is without sin among you, let him first cast a stone at her** (v. 7).

Don't speak evil of your brother lest you be condemned. Notice Jesus wrote in the dirt, not in stone as He did with the Law of Moses. He was saying, "Don't be hardhearted; be merciful and forgiving." Jude said hardhearted people

---

[3]*The Modern Language Bible, The New Berkeley Version in Modern English* (Grand Rapids, MI: Zondervan, 1969).

are not afraid to speak evil of dignities. (vv. 8,10). Speaking against God's anointed will stop the flow of the anointing in one's life. Oh, how we must learn not to accuse, malign and hurt one another with our tongues.

Ephesians 4:29 says, **Let no corrupt communication proceed out of your mouth, but that which is good to the use of edifying, that it may minister grace unto the hearers.**

Malice

This brings us to the final aspect mentioned by Paul in Ephesians 4:31: malice. Malice is the inflicting of evil upon someone with the deliberate intent to cause harm. It is having ill will toward someone to the extent of cursing them.

We are called to bless people. Malice leads to cursing people and causes one to do things out of spite. Those who become malicious don't realize it, but maliciousness leads to malignancy. It is rebellion against God. Malice is such an atrocity, because it goes against the loving, forbearing, gracious nature of God. It is also viewed severely by God because it is intentional and premeditated.

With it, we are taking judgment into our own hands and setting up our own kingdoms. Like a malignant tumor, it goes off on its own and spreads throughout the body.

Just as the natural body cannot allow a malignancy to go unchecked, God cannot allow malice to go unchecked. Malice is rebellion of the worst sort against God. Those who continually operate in malice will surely be cut off.

There will always be people who want to keep rehearsing the past. They want to remember the bitterness, pain and hardships of segregation and even the hypocrisy of this present generation. How long shall we mourn and how often must we recall?

Jesus Christ bore the sin of racism and prejudice on the cross 2,000 years ago. It was buried with Him. He was raised from the dead to be the firstfruits of a new race of people who had never existed before (1 Corinthians 15:23). The funeral service for racism has lasted too long. Let the dead bury the dead, but let us go on to follow Christ.

Again, let us remember the words of the apostle Paul in Ephesians 4:32. It says:

And be ye kind one to another, tenderhearted, forgiving one another, even as God for Christ's sake hath forgiven you.

But you may say, "How can I do that when there is so much injustice and I have had so many bad experiences?"

The next verse, Ephesians 5:1, says:

Be ye therefore followers of God, as dear children.

The key is to become as children — having a childlike disposition. Let's see what the Word says about this.

8

Heirs Together of God's Grace

We Must Become as Children

To avoid malice, we must become as children. Notice Paul's words in First Corinthians 14:20:

> Be not children in understanding: howbeit in malice be ye children....

Growing up as a child in Little Rock, Arkansas, I can remember sometimes riding the old city bus with my mother. Before the advent of malls, everybody shopped downtown.

I recall seeing different provisions made in the stores for White people and Colored people. When Mama took me to eat at the old Woolworth store, there was one counter labeled "White" and one labeled "Colored."

One thing that always stood out in my mind, even as a young child, was how we children kept looking at each other. When a White parent would see her child gazing across the invisible fence, she would reach down and turn the child's face away. With a mild admonishment, she seemed to be saying, "Don't even think about fellowshipping with that kid." When being led out the door, the child would almost invariably have a baffled look on his face, as if saying to me, "I don't understand this — do you?"

There was one specific incident that I will never forget.

Mama had taken me to the clinic. On the way home we stopped by a candy counter and got some of those candied orange slices. (They were my favorite!) I was carrying my little sack of candy as we went outside and got into position to catch the city bus.

When we got on the bus, a White child was sitting on the front seat with his mother. While Mama was taking care of the fare, the little boy and I were staring at each other and smiling. He had a little toy truck to play with, and I had a sack of orange slices. So we did what came naturally: he held out his truck to me and I offered him an orange slice.

As we reached out to each other, I could see his mother getting anxious, knowing the naiveté of these two children but also knowing the reproach of racial mixing.

Then he turned to his mother and said, "Mom, can he sit with me?" She carefully but quickly pulled him up next to her, whispered to him and gave me a stern look.

Mama grabbed my hand and we went to the back of the bus. As we were walking away, I heard that little boy begin to cry. Getting louder, he said, "Mom, why can't we play?" She finally had to spank him to quiet him down.

Then I asked Mama, "How come we can't sit together and play?"

She said, "You're too young to understand, but I pray to God that one day it won't be like this."

Mama was right — I *didn't* understand. Neither did the little White boy. Like the apostle Paul had said, we were children in understanding. We were naive. We were too innocent and pure in our hearts at that time to know the difference in ethnic groups.

All we knew was that we were children, and children like to play. He had a toy; I had some candy. We were children in understanding, but we were also as children in malice. There was no ill will or evil thinking in our hearts toward each other. We had not been indoctrinated with racial prejudice. Neither of us had experienced anything that would cause us to become embittered or angry. We had no malice.

Children are that way. They don't have time for malice. Playing and having fun are too important for them to be sitting around with malice in their hearts. Children can fight one moment and be playing together the next. It's amazing how quickly they forgive and how tender their little hearts are.

No wonder Jesus said:

Except ye be converted, and become as little children, ye shall not enter into the kingdom of heaven.

And whoso shall receive one such little child in my name receiveth me.

Matthew 18:3,5

God loves innocence of heart, pure motives and goodwill. Jesus said, **Blessed are the pure in heart: for they shall see God** (Matthew 5:8).

The greatest ones in the kingdom are those who have childlike hearts. We too must become as little children. As Paul said, **...in malice be ye children** (1 Corinthians 14:20).

In that situation from my childhood, we couldn't help it that our parents did not get along. We couldn't help it that there were ignorant laws on the books that segregated the races.

Don't Keep Worrying About the Past

I thank God that, in spite of all the evils of society, I have been able to maintain an innocent heart when it comes to racial relations. Riding in the back of the bus, drinking at separate fountains, eating at separate counters — these are not fighting words to me.

I am not naive enough to believe that every White person loves me or means me well. Neither am I naive enough to think that racism and prejudice don't exist. But I choose to remain the way I was as a child on that bus in Little Rock almost four decades ago. I want to have a forgiving spirit, to think good rather than evil, to see people's hearts rather than their skin, to respect their faith and not their person.

There are too many exciting, positive and wonderful things to do than to sit around thinking about things done 200 years ago by some ignorant people. We can't keep worrying about the past. Neither should we waste time worrying about people who, even today, are ignorant about racial matters.

As the apostle Paul said:

> **But if any man be ignorant, let him be ignorant** (or ignorant).
>
> **1 Corinthians 14:38**

In other words, if any man continues to act as though he is ignorant after being informed, let him be ignored or looked over when it comes to spiritual manifestations.

People who refuse to change will be left behind and will not participate in this next move of God. God will ignore or pass over them.

"In Understanding Be Men"

While our attitude must be childlike, it is time that we grow up in knowledge. When the subject of sex is brought up at church, Christians blush and become uncomfortable. The same is true when frank discussions about ethnic issues arise: We get uncomfortable and start squirming in our seats. We want to pretend that these are not realities and, like our treatment of sex, we play little children's games.

On the old TV show, *The Beverly Hillbillies*, Uncle Jed was always saying about Jethro: "One o' these days I'm gonna have a long talk with that boy." Having grown up in the hills of Tennessee, Jethro was naive about the facts of life.

Sometimes when I see some of the blunders that my brothers and sisters make in racial matters, I feel like Uncle Jed.

Likewise, too many Christians are sitting around talking about the "birds and bees" of race relations instead of having good, frank discussions. As the apostle Paul said in First Corinthians 14:20:

> **...in understanding be men.**

Let's take a look at this in the Word and see how we can grow up in this area.

Ignorance — Mother of Prejudice

We just quoted a portion of First Corinthians 14:20. Let's look at the entire verse:

> **Brethren, be not children in understanding: howbeit in malice be ye children, but in understanding be men.**

One of the biggest perpetrators of prejudice is ignorance. Many people are ignorant — whether uninformed or misinformed — about those of other ethnic groups. As one brother put it, "What we're not up on, we're down on."

Some people are down on other races because they don't know them. There are some who don't intend to behave improperly toward others; they are just ignorant about what to do. Even when trying to reach out, they end up offending people or condescending to the point of turning people off. They "overdo it." So while no malice is intended and these people are basically innocent in heart, their heads are not where they should be.

The answer to ignorance is knowledge. We must study in order to gain knowledge. To be motivated to study, we must care enough about the subject to spend the time.

In matters of diplomacy, our State Department goes to great lengths to make sure that the customs of other countries are honored during official visits. This is to ensure that the other country is not offended by a show of disrespect. The fact that an attempt is made to respect custom and protocol is a sign of honor.

On the other hand, failure to acknowledge the customs of others is a reproach which can break or hinder effective communication and relationships. When we do this, it comes across as arrogant and high-minded.

Comparing the Husband/Wife Relationship With Race Relations

Notice these words from the apostle Peter:

> **Likewise, ye husbands, dwell with them according to knowledge, giving honour unto the wife, as unto the weaker vessel, and as being heirs together of the grace of life; that your prayers be not hindered.**
> **1 Peter 3:7**

Now I know that we normally use this Scripture verse to teach on husband/wife relationships, but I believe it can be expanded to address other relationships as well, including those of different races.

Peter is telling the husband not to be ignorant of his wife, or of the feminine gender as a whole. He is to dwell with her according to knowledge. You cannot dwell with someone harmoniously unless you know them. This means that a man should understand the husband/wife relationship; he should know about women in general and his own wife, in particular.

Peter equates this with giving honor. To deem something or someone as not worthy of study is to deem it or them as dishonorable or not worthy of respect.

Notice Peter goes on to say, **...giving honour...as unto the weaker vessel**. This term *weaker vessel* speaks of the qualities of being delicate, sensitive and weaker in strength. It also speaks of relative position in terms of covenant.[1]

Peter says that the husband must study to know his wife in order to honor her as a delicate, sensitive, fragile vessel and as one having the "minority" position in the covenant. How does this apply to racial and ethnic relations?

For the reader's edification, when the term *minority* is used, it is not speaking of inferiority or lesser in equality. Men are not superior to women; Whites are not superior to Blacks innately. The man only has the authority because he was formed before the woman (1 Timothy 2:13). The woman achieves equality, not by usurping authority, but by submitting as unto the Lord (Ephesians 5:22). The point is not really meant to show superiority or equality, but how these roles relate to each other in terms of knowledge and treatment. The husband and wife, and all of God's children, are heirs together of the grace of life. When we say *majority*, we are not speaking of personage, but of culture mores.

Majority vs. Minority

It is a principle that those who are in the majority position tend to be ignorant and insensitive toward those in the minority. Men are often accused in today's culture of being "male chauvinists" for their attitudes toward women. They say things that stereotype or classify all women the same. Oftentimes males presume superiority and make patronizing or condescending statements.

---

[1]Strong, "Greek Dictionary of New Testament Words," p. 16, #772, and p. 65, #4599.

Because it is a "man's world," women have been trained in studying males and learning how to please their husbands, who are considered dominant or the majority. This was particularly true in Peter's day.

Before Christ, women were considered as nothing more than property. They were not even counted in the census and were left out of most genealogies as though they really did not exist.

With the coming of Christ, the message was changed to one of equality between men and women. In the beginning Adam and Eve were one, heirs together of the creation of God. In fact, both Adam and Eve were called Adam (Genesis 5:2).

Peter was trying here to enjoin these saints to come out of the old system of looking down on females and begin to honor them as equals. But he also understood that he was in a society where literature, philosophy and religion only featured the male majority. Women knew how to dwell with the men, but men knew precious little about the women.

This same attitude must be applied to races today. Because the White race is the majority race in America, everyone is familiar with its customs, mannerisms and language. Minorities have had to learn this if they were indeed going to be able to operate in the system.

If a Black tells another Black, "You are trying to talk 'proper,'" this means, "You are talking like a White person."

The standards for success and excellence have been perceived by what the majority race does. So, in essence, minorities have been passively forced to learn the ways of the majority in order to fit in and gain acceptance. On the positive hand, it has been easier for minorities to learn the ways of the majority because the majority culture is prevalent, in areas such as media and education.

Conversely, those in the majority, without the benefit of media and other means of exposure, must study to know minorities. If they are to dwell with minorities according to knowledge, they cannot learn passively; they must do it purposely and deliberately, like the males that Peter exhorted in his day. They had to stop acting as though their wives were just property or servants relegated to menial tasks and having to walk three steps behind their husbands.

Show Honor and Respect

Today's major ethnic group must take time to know its fellow man. In spite of the relative position in which people may find themselves, they are yet equal. We must dwell with each other according to knowledge — not stereotypes.

As I have found, there are many good men who are not good husbands because they don't know how to relate to their wives. Likewise, there are many good people with innocent hearts who fail at racial relations because they lack understanding. They don't know how to dwell together according to knowledge. Without thinking, they presume superiority, make statements and do offensive things without really meaning to. Although Paul was dealing with a different subject, I say, as he said to the church at Corinth, **...I would not have you ignorant** (1 Corinthians 12:1).

Like American missionaries who go to foreign countries and begin Americanizing everything, sometimes dominant cultures tend to base acceptance of minorities on how much those minorities act like them.

I have heard some dear brothers say, "I like him — he's a good Black." What they really mean is: "He acts more like we do than the stereotypical Black."

This reeks of tokenism and control. It's like saying, "If we're going to have Black people around here, we're going to choose them."

Either knowingly or unknowingly, this system of approving some members of a race while rejecting others can create strife and tension within that minority race and foster a caste or class system.

Many more sensitive Blacks take offense to this, especially those who are more prone to retain original cultural characteristics and practices.

In other words, majority groups must learn to be less critical with minorities who don't fit their preconceived idea of what is acceptable. Care must be taken not to label more assertive minorities as "uppity." Prejudice may cause Whites to call the assertiveness of a White brother "boldness" while calling the assertiveness of a Black brother "arrogance."

This is a common complaint I received in discussions with Blacks while gathering material for this book. We must not confuse personality with character. Many misconceptions can be avoided if we learn to dwell according to knowledge and give honor as unto the weaker vessel.

We must understand that minorities are going to naturally be more sensitive in the area of culture and racial semantics. This has been brought about by years of social stigmatization, rejection and discrimination. It is important to be sensitive without being sensational, to condescend without a condescending attitude, to be appreciative without being patronizing. These well-intentioned measures may become turnoffs if one does not have a good knowledge of another's culture.

The most important point to remember about what the apostle Peter said is to give honor. Respect is essential to any healthy relationship. Peter says respect comes from the realization that we are heirs together of God's grace. If we do not respect one another, then we frustrate the grace of God and our prayers are hindered (1 Peter 3:7).

When a husband mistreats his wife and takes advantage of her because she is the weaker vessel, it hinders God's blessing on his life. The same thing happens when a majority race shows disrespect for another race.

The law of Christ always requires the last to be first and the first to be last (Matthew 19:30). The apostle Paul said that upon the unseemly parts there is bestowed the more abundant honor (1 Corinthians 12:23). If not, the grace of God (the Anointing) is hindered.

Under Christianity, the wife does not walk behind the husband. On the contrary, the husband opens the door for the wife. Under Christianity, the attitude should always be "ladies first."

So the minority position receives the most honor under the law of the Anointing. This is dwelling according to knowledge. We are talking not about privilege but about honor. *Honor is learned so that respect can be earned.*

If Any Man Lack Knowledge...

Brethren, concerning ethnic relations, God would not have us ignorant!

If you lack knowledge in this area, ask!

Let God hook you up with someone from another race and culture, so you can learn from one another.

As mentioned earlier, minorities typically know and understand the ways of the majority culture because of exposure. But, as a rule, minority culture tends to be ignored by the majority except in the negative sense.

After finding a friend from another culture for whom you have honor and respect, ask questions about things you don't understand. Then expect candid and honest answers, even correction where needed.

You cannot help it if you have never been exposed to other cultures and therefore have no understanding. As long as you have a pure heart and are sincere, people will accept you and God will approve you.

Earlier in this study, I mentioned my relationship with Happy Caldwell. I can honestly say that Happy is one of the purest and most sincere men I have ever known. He is so quick to repent and so sensitive to the Holy Spirit. His innocence borders on "sanctified naiveté."

With a highly integrated congregation, Happy is often faced with situations regarding culture in which he has had no experience. He will sometimes call me, and we will discuss what is happening in a situation and why Blacks respond or react in a certain way. He asks because he honestly wants to know so that he can do the right thing and be a good pastor. He despises hypocrisy and pretense, and he desires genuineness in every relationship. He lets me speak honestly and candidly regarding these matters. As Scripture says:

> **Iron sharpeneth iron; so a man sharpeneth the countenance of his friend.**
>
> **Proverbs 27:17**

He likewise speaks to me about matters of which he has knowledge and experience. How valuable are such relationships in gaining understanding and learning to dwell together according to knowledge. As Psalm 133 says, God will command His blessing where brethren dwell together in unity.

Learn Ethnic History and Culture

Another means of dwelling together according to knowledge is by studying the culture and history of others. Respect comes through knowledge of accomplishment. It is good that those from other cultures are made aware of the contributions and accomplishments of others. Care must be taken not to let this become a diversion (as some have become overly occupied). But if used lawfully, much benefit can be derived.

There are several excellent books available now that give balanced, scholarly information on this subject.

The Israelites were admonished by God to teach their children about their heritage so that it could be passed on from generation to generation. This was not meant to establish some doctrine of superiority but to establish esteem, respect and identity within their culture in order to preserve it.

Satan has always desired to extinguish ethnic groups from the earth, especially the Jewish people. But God will not permit the elimination of any race. He created them and He will sustain them.

It is wrong to suppress or hold back information about minority contributions to history as though it is not significant. On the other hand, ethnic history should not supersede or replace national history in terms of importance. Similarly, contributions of people of color in the Bible or in church history should not be exalted above the overall view of the Scriptures. As we have already mentioned, Christ is the focus of the Scriptures and the Church.

The heritage factor is important in establishing respect in a multicultural society. It is also important to mix with other cultures in common experiences.

Understanding Brings the Anointing

When congregations worship together or receive ministry from those of a different ethnic group, it brings understanding and enlightenment. When the order and organization of a White congregation meets the fervor and emotion of a Black congregation, there is a mutual exchange and a powerful flow of the corporate anointing.

Over a period of time, we pick up things from one another. Soon you cannot distinguish between the singing voices of the Whites from the Blacks. The White brothers and sisters pick up on the Black lingo. Before you know it, there is a respect and appreciation for how each group worships God. The common denominator is the Word. **Faith cometh by hearing, and hearing by the word of God** (Romans 10:17).

So, we can dwell with one another according to knowledge, as heirs together of God's anointing. Ignorance need not be an excuse. Here are some things we are to do:

1. We should establish fellowship with a brother or sister of another culture who will speak frankly to us, and who allows us to ask questions when we don't understand.

2. We should study good books or listen to tapes in order to learn of the contributions of other cultures and understand their customs.

3. We should mix with people of other cultures in common experiences, such as worship, so that the anointing can be shared.

Then we can experience, as Peter said, what it means to be heirs together of the grace and anointing of God, and nothing will hinder it.

9

Where to From Here?

As we look ahead to the twenty-first century, we should be aware that the Lord Himself prophesies an increase in ethnic tension. Both at home in America and abroad, dividing lines which so many have toiled so hard to erase will reappear more pronounced than ever.

Neither the lure of trade and economic viability through treaties like GATT, nor common-defense treaties like the one signed by NATO, nor international police agencies like the United Nations shall be able to deal with the poison of hatred in the heart of man.

Unless there is a mighty outpouring of the Holy Spirit with people endeavoring to walk in love, we may see a blood bath likened to nothing this world has ever known.

I have been particularly concerned with what seems to be a more pronounced swing toward extremism in America. Not only are racial tensions heightening, but there is a gender war as well.

Politically, at the time of this writing, there has been a swing toward conservatism, with Republicans holding majorities in both houses of Congress and the state governorships. The fact that there has been a swing toward conservatism is not alarming but quite expected. America has been moving in that direction for some time now.

But what *is* alarming is how some people are interpreting this swing. Already, they are saying things like,

"It's the return of the White male" and "The White male fights back!" This is dangerous language.

Signals are going out into the Black community that "Jim Crow" is on its way back.

Many Blacks, especially the more elderly who tend to be staunch Democrats, are fearful of seeing a return of the days of old.

The young, more radical Blacks on the streets are saying, "Not without a fight! We will die first before we go back to that!"

Fueled by relentless talk shows, sound bites and editorials that give no hint of compromise or moderation, many minorities fear that they are being backed into a corner. With these feelings, the result is usually a fight.

The Church Must Take a Stand

The body of Christ must recognize what Satan would like to accomplish through all of this. With the mandate of less governmental interference, we will more and more be at the mercy of the moral conscience and goodwill of the people.

Less governmental regulation in commerce, education and the private sector is a scary proposition to minorities. When it comes to Civil Rights, the government has been their strongest advocate. While most minorities agree that there has been too much dependence on government as advocate, helper and counselor, there is a skepticism toward the private sector "doing the right thing" for any sustained period of time.

In a country dominated by profit motive and business acumen rather than moral and spiritual excellence, these fears may be well-founded. After all, profit was the real motive behind Christians owning slaves. They quoted Scriptures but also counted the money — all in one breath.

After all, they would say, those savages were better off being the slaves of Christians than being free heathen.

Most minorities sense this same spirit today in a more sophisticated package. They fear the conservatives are using religion as a cloak to "do what's right" for these minorities.

Just as conservatives are appalled at the government presuming to know what is best for the people, minorities are appalled at suburban White folks presuming to know what is best for minorities.

This political diversity will be the next big issue with which the Church will have to come to grips. If the Church does not wake up and deal with these perceptions, the result will be a divided Church.

Why do I say we must deal with the perceptions?

As one man said, perception is more powerful than truth. It is how one perceives a thing that makes it "truth" to him or her.

When minorities see the so-called "Christian Right" teaming up with conservative politicians to form coalitions, it gives off a perception of endorsement. These conservative Christians passionately fight for things like family values, the lives of the unborn and lower taxes. Yet these same people did not "feel led" to get involved in the Civil Rights Movement. It was the liberal Christians who showed up and even died to advance Civil Rights and to overthrow oppression.

This is one of the primary reasons that the majority of traditional Black churches espouse liberal political views while being conservative on moral issues. This rather strange combination of political liberalism and moral conservatism has been prevalent because these churches have formed the basic hub of leadership in the Black community.

They have served as the "community centers" not only for worship but for most other community issues, including social and political ones. The church has been the one piece of property the people owned and its pastor was the one leader whom they elected. Because the pastor was articulate, he generally became the social leader and in many cases was quite involved in politics, particularly Civil Rights issues.

The result of all this has been an increasing gap between the traditional Black church and the conservative, evangelical church. In fact, it is almost as though the two are in different worlds.

The level of distrust and suspicion among these traditional Black churches and evangelicals exceeds what most Christians could ever imagine.

As I mentioned earlier, with the conservative swing of the pendulum in the last election, this gap will only increase and become more pronounced.

If the evangelical churches do not adjust themselves to the new sociopolitical order of less government, fewer social programs, welfare reform and greater local autonomy, we may have the race war of all race wars!

Evangelical churches cannot sit back as they did during the Civil Rights Movement and miss out on one of the most massive transitions in American history. Christ was not known as "the affiliate of the rich, powerful and privileged." He was the Friend of the poor, humble and underclassed.

Although the media bears much of the blame for the image the "Christian Right" has been given — as hypocritical, guileful, self-righteous — much of that reputation has been earned.

Just as a geopolitical nation like the United States must have foreign-relations policies, ethnic nations must have them as well. The policy of the evangelical church world has been to "send money overseas but ignore thy neighbor next door."

As evangelicals, we pride ourselves on being doctrinally sound and the advancers of the Gospel. But in being doctrinally sound, we violate the most important law of Scripture. In our zeal for evangelism we violate its first principle.

Love Your Neighbor as Yourself

Let's consider this passage of Scripture:

And, behold, a certain lawyer stood up, and tempted him, saying, Master, what shall I do to inherit eternal life?

He said unto him, What is written in the law? how readest thou?

And he answering said, Thou shalt love the Lord thy God with all thy heart, and with all thy soul, and with all thy strength, and with all thy mind; and thy neighbour as thyself.

And he said unto him, Thou hast answered right: this do, and thou shalt live.

But he, willing to justify himself, said unto Jesus, And who is my neighbour?

And Jesus answering said, A certain man went down from Jerusalem to Jericho, and fell among thieves, which stripped him of his raiment, and wounded him, and departed, leaving him half dead.

And by chance there came down a certain priest that way: and when he saw him, he passed by on the other side.

And likewise a Levite, when he was at the place, came and looked on him, and passed by on the other side.

But a certain Samaritan, as he journeyed, came where he was: and when he saw him, he had compassion on him,

And went to him, and bound up his wounds, pouring in oil and wine, and set him on his own beast, and brought him to an inn, and took care of him.

And on the morrow when he departed, he took out two pence, and gave them to the host, and said unto him, Take care of him; and whatsoever thou spendest more, when I come again, I will repay thee.

Which now of these three, thinkest thou, was neighbour unto him that fell among the thieves?

And he said, He that shewed mercy on him. Then said Jesus unto him, Go, and do thou likewise.

Luke 10:25-37

Notice that in this scenario the lawyer (the fundamentalist) wanted to know what must be done to inherit eternal life. Then he, being a Bible believer, answered his own question by giving the Great Commandment of Scripture:

Love God with all your heart and your neighbor as yourself (author's paraphrase).

But then this question came up as the lawyer sought to justify himself: **Who is my neighbour?**

Jesus goes on to describe how a man from Jerusalem fell among thieves and the religious people distanced themselves from him — walking on the other side of the road. The priest and Levite were devout conservatives no doubt on their way to church to give in the missions offering. Then a Samaritan passed by.

Samaritans were a people of whom Jesus Himself said, **Ye worship ye know not what...** (John 4:22). This Samaritan did instinctively what the Great Commandment required, without actually knowing the Law. He was a "liberal," but he was a doer of the Word.

A Time of Transition

My first and greatest concern is that the evangelical church world will pass by on the "other side" during this crucial, transitional period. It is absolutely essential that the body of Christ pull together and set the example for race relations.

Secondly, African-American churches, especially Word churches, must realize that they will suddenly be thrust into the leadership role in the Afro-American community. The old, traditional, liberal leadership will fall by the wayside in this transition to conservatism.

People will have to be taught self-sufficiency and how to believe God rather than continuing to lean upon the government. Word churches have been strategically raised up by God for this hour.

Recent polls have indicated that organizations like the NAACP and the Black Caucus are no longer being looked to as leaders of the African-American community. A new brand of leader is now coming forth to steer the people into this new era. We can ill afford to spend our time pursuing doctrines that are unprofitable.

Satan wants to divert our attention from preparing for this awesome responsibility of leading our communities and congregations into the twenty-first century. Things will be vastly different then from the way they are today.

The cold war between liberalism and conservatism is over. Liberalism as we know it is dead. Black people must realize that they have come out of their "Egypt," and it's time for them to go into the "promised land." The government will not be able to fight the "giants" this time. The "giant" to which I am referring is unbelief — failure to depend totally and completely upon God. The battlefield is not in the streets of South Central Los Angeles but in our own minds.

As affirmative actions, quota requirements and various consent decrees go by the wayside, people must be taught that *God* has an affirmative-action program. It is the Word of God in our mouths, called confession. The body of Christ must operate in the principles of reconciliation and fulfill the law of Christ.

Thirdly, we must realize that during this time of transition, there is going to be opportunity for strife and division. We must endeavor to keep the unity of the Spirit in the bond of peace (Ephesians 4:3). We must walk worthy of our vocation, which is ensuring the flow of the corporate anointing (Ephesians 4:1). We must make sure that we do not preach out of contention and that we follow after things making for peace (Philippians 1:16; Romans 14:19).

Fourthly, we must be as children in regard to malice, but in understanding be mature. As shown in the example from my childhood that was given earlier, children are innocent in heart because they have not yet learned to discriminate. They do not see color first the way adults do; they see the heart. Galatians 3:28 says:

There is neither Jew nor Greek, there is neither bond nor free, there is neither male nor female: for ye are all one in Christ Jesus.

We Must Come Together as One

In Christ, there is no distinction, no discrimination of ethnic group, color, sex or social status. As we eliminate carnality, fleshly pursuits and indulgences, we will walk in this revelation: In Christ, we are all equal.

Although there are no distinctions in Christ, we are members in particular. Not all members have the same function. We must therefore learn to dwell with one another according to knowledge. To be mature, we must understand, appreciate and permit the function of every part of the body of Christ. This requires us to know one another and to respect one another — regardless of race.

Yes, in the last days there will be wars and rumors of wars, nation against nation and kingdom against kingdom. Jesus prophesied it, so we know it is accurate.

But as the rest of the world follows Satan and his diversionary tactics, we in the body of Christ will not be diverted.

We can accept one another's diversity and appreciate the uniqueness of everyone without becoming diverted.

Diversions lead to receding or pulling away from others. It is Satan's way of weakening the Church. Once we begin to recede, the next step is to secede — to completely withdraw or break away from others. Though we started at the same place — in Christ — Satan wants us to take divergent paths, dividing us into religious, political and ethnic camps.

Redeemed From the Curse!

Finally, we must remain doctrinally sound. We must continue in the things we have learned, avoiding strange doctrines. We must not allow emotions and feelings to dictate what we do or how we respond. We can only do what the Word says to do. If it is not in the Word, we will not do it.

There is no justification in God's Word for segregation or racism in the Church.

Christ fulfilled the promise of a pure seed coming through the lineage of the Jewish people. The Jews became God's people by promise — not by preference. After Christ, there was no need for a middle wall of partition. It has been taken down by Christ. We must not be beguiled from the simplicity that is in Christ Jesus.

In Christ, all who believe are Abraham's seed. In Christ, we were redeemed from the curse of the Law (Galatians 3:13). We do not have to trace our genealogy to determine whether we are cursed or blessed.

It is fallacious teaching which says all the descendants of Ham (Black people) were cursed. The truth is, all were cursed, **for all have sinned, and come short of the glory of God** (Romans 3:23). The good news is that Christ has redeemed us from *every* curse. There is no need to make it complicated. Christ, the Anointed One, is the end of all strife regarding genealogies.

Our God — A God of Diversity

As we look at the final book of the Bible, the book of Revelation, we find that God is a God of diversity. Every nation, kindred and tongue will be represented in heaven. It is interesting that when John describes the glory of God the Father, he names five different colors. In Revelation 4:1-3 he says:

> **After this I looked, and, behold, a door was opened in heaven: and the first voice which I heard was as it were of a trumpet talking with me; which said, Come up hither, and I will shew thee things which must be hereafter.**
>
> **And immediately I was in the spirit: and, behold, a throne was set in heaven, and one sat on the throne.**
>
> **And he that sat was to look upon like a jasper and a sardine stone: and there was a rainbow round about the throne, in sight like unto an emerald.**

Although only three stones are mentioned here, they are composed of five colors — red, yellow, brown, black and white — the skin colors of all the different people of the world. No group can lay any exclusive claim on God. He is a God of diversity with a diverse people.

As long as we keep Christ and His anointing as the central theme and focus of all we do, we can have *diversity without diversion.*

Conclusion

I will conclude the book by saying in a nutshell that the greatest obstacle for Blacks to overcome in being reconciled to Whites is *trust;* the greatest obstacle for Whites to overcome in being reconciled to Blacks is *respect.*

Trust and *respect* — they both must be earned, but they both will come as a result of our diligently endeavoring to dwell together in unity.

As we prepare to enter into the greatest revival our world has ever known, it is imperative that we allow nothing to hinder the anointing. We must come into unity for the Anointing's sake; and, in Jesus' name, we will do it. I call every minister, lay leader and saint of God to be reconciled to one another.

If you are serious about putting this issue to rest, join me in this prayer:

Heavenly Father, I thank You that Jesus has torn down the walls that separated the races. I confess that the races are of one blood and in Christ, and we are of one Spirit. I bind division, strife, contention and malice, and I loose the anointing of peace to flow according to Psalm 133. I decree it done, in Jesus' name. Amen!

About the Author

Silas Johnson is a pastor and teacher. He is Senior Pastor of Full Counsel Christian Fellowship, a thriving congregation of 1,500 in North Little Rock, Arkansas, from which he and his wife Jennifer have a vision for reaching the world for Christ. An international speaker, Pastor Johnson is known for his ability to teach the Word of God in depth but with a simplistic, humorous and down-to-earth style.

Referred to by one minister as a "statesman," Pastor Johnson is used by the Lord to provide insight and direction to the Body of Christ through sharing the mind of God. His balanced, line-upon-line teaching with an emphasis on *faith* establishes God's people, inspiring and challenging them to live responsible, overcoming and victorious lives.

In addition, the Lord uses Pastor Johnson in the media ministry. The radio programs, *Thus Saith The Lord* and *Oracles Of The Air*, are broadcast daily in several markets. The *Arm Of The Lord* television program is aired throughout Arkansas. Pastor Johnson is also president of the Joshua Broadcasting (radio) Network.

The Johnsons reside in Sherwood, Arkansas, and have five children — four sons and one daughter.

To contact Silas Johnson,
write:

Silas Johnson
Full Counsel Ministries
P. O. Box 2160
North Little Rock, Arkansas 72115

*Please include your prayer requests
and comments when you write.*

Additional copies of this book
are available from your local bookstore.

HARRISON HOUSE
Tulsa, Oklahoma 74153

In Canada,
books are available from:

Word Alive
P. O. Box 670
Niverville, Manitoba
CANADA R0A 1E0

The Harrison House Vision

Proclaiming the truth and the power
Of the Gospel of Jesus Christ
With excellence;

Challenging Christians to
Live victoriously,
Grow spiritually,
Know God intimately.